Scotland's leading educational publishers

D0512934

Higher
MODERN STUDIES
GRADE A BOOSTER

© 2017 Leckie & Leckie Ltd

001/16022017

10 9 8 7 6 5 4 3 2 1

ISBN 9780007590889

Published by
Leckie & Leckie Ltd
An imprint of HarperCollins*Publishers*
Westerhill Road, Bishopbriggs, Glasgow, G64 2QT
T: 0844 576 8126   F: 0844 576 8131
leckieandleckie@harpercollins.co.uk
www.leckieandleckie.co.uk

Commissioning Editor: Katherine Wilkinson
Managing Editor: Craig Balfour

Special thanks to
Janice McNeillie (copy edit)
Louise Robb (proofread)
Jouve (layout)
Ink Tank (cover)

Printed and bound in China by RR Donnelley APS

A CIP Catalogue record for this book is available from the British Library.

Acknowledgements

Twitter image on page 7 © Bloomicon / Shutterstock.com, all other images © Shutterstock.com

General marking principles and questions adapted from SQA past papers reproduced with permission, copyright © Scottish Qualifi cations Authority.

Graph on page 77 from *Referendum briefing: child poverty in Scotland* by Hannah Aldridge and Peter Kenway, published in 2014 by the Joseph Rowntree Foundation. Reproduced by permission of the Joseph Rowntree Foundation.

Graph on page 79 by the National Consortium for the Study of Terrorism and Responses to Terrorism (START). (2016). Global Terrorism Database [Data file]. Retrieved from https://www.start.umd.edu/gtd.

Article on page 116, *What Better Together learned too late*, reproduced by permission of the New Statesman.

Whilst every effort has been made to trace the copyright holders, in cases where this has been unsuccessful, or if any have inadvertently been overlooked, the Publishers would gladly receive any information enabling them to rectify any error or omission at the first opportunity.

CONTENTS

Introduction

What will I study in Higher Modern Studies?

You will find out at the beginning of the school year the Course Units your teacher has chosen to study with you. The Higher Modern Studies syllabus is shown below:

- Democracy in Scotland and the United Kingdom.
- Social Issues in the UK: EITHER Social Inequality OR Crime and the Law.
- International Issues: EITHER a World Power OR World Issue.

For the International Issues section, your focus of study will either be on a G20 country e.g. USA, China, South Africa, Brazil, Germany, India etc, or a contemporary world issue such as Terrorism, Worldwide Poverty, Child Soldiers, Nuclear Proliferation, Economic Crisis, or the Effects of War.

How is the Higher Modern Studies course assessed?

The Modern Studies exam involves two components which are both externally assessed by the Scottish Qualifications Authority (SQA). During term time you will complete an assignment. You will choose an issue to research and complete a report. This will be written under controlled conditions as set out by the SQA and the school will send your work to the SQA to be assessed. The second component of the examination is a question paper which will ask you to write extended responses as well as answer source-based questions. The exam diet begins around the end of April each year until the beginning of June. The Modern Studies exam will be scheduled sometime during the exam diet. The allocation of marks is as follows:

- Assignment 30 marks (1/3 of total grade)
- Question Paper 60 marks (2/3 of total grade)
- Total 90 marks

How will this book help me?

You will find certain parts of this Grade Booster book helpful at different times of the school year. For example, when you are carrying out research for your coursework, refer to the Assignment chapter. This book is not designed for you to read in one go. Once your teacher has introduced you to certain exam skills, refer to the appropriate section of the book. This book will guide you through how to answer the different types of questions in the exam as well as carry out your research for the assignment.

What else can I do to be prepared for assessments?

It is important you are prepared for the year ahead and the course content you are about to study. Unlike other school subjects Modern Studies pupils are constantly exposed to the course content since social media and the internet can be used to support your studies.

Once you know the Units you will study in Higher Modern Studies, you can begin to become familiar with current events and debates surrounding the topic. The easiest way to do this is to use the internet and social media. Following Twitter and Facebook pages are a very convenient way of keeping yourself up to date. When checking in with your friends on Facebook or Twitter you will be able to read about Modern Studies issues at the same time. So in a way, you will be carrying out research without even having to go out of your way to do so. You could also check websites on a regular basis too. But make sure you keep a record of useful sources and copy the URL so you can access the information at a later date. This will come in VERY handy when you begin your research for your assignment.

Below is a list of recommended pages on the internet or social media which you can follow, as well as the associated relevant Unit of study:

Key Facebook pages

Source	Type of source	Relevant Unit of study
The Independent	Newspaper	Democracy in Scotland and the UK; Social Inequality; Crime and the Law; World Powers; World Issues
The Guardian	Newspaper	Democracy in Scotland and the UK; Social Inequality; Crime and the Law; World Powers; World Issues
The Telegraph	Newspaper	Democracy in Scotland and the UK; Social Inequality; Crime and the Law; World Powers; World Issues

(**continued**)

Source	Type of source	Relevant Unit of study
Channel 4 News	News broadcaster	Democracy in Scotland and the UK; Social Inequality; Crime and the Law; World Powers; World Issues
Scottish Parliament	Government	Democracy in Scotland and the UK; Social Inequality; Crime and the Law
Joseph Rowntree Foundation	Non-profit organisation	Social Inequality
Prison Reform Trust	Non-profit organisation	Crime and the Law
Police Scotland	Public organisation	Crime and the Law
Families Outside	Non-profit organisation	Crime and the Law
BBC	News broadcaster	Democracy in Scotland and the UK; Social Inequality; Crime and the Law; World Powers; World Issues
BBC World Service	News broadcaster	World Powers; World Issues
BBC Africa	News broadcaster	World Issues; World Powers
The Economist	Magazine	Social Inequalities; World Powers; World Issues
Al Jazeera	News broadcaster	World Issues
The Economist Asia	Magazine	World Power – China; World Issues
CNN	News broadcaster	World Power – USA; World Issues
Fox News	News broadcaster	World Power – USA; World Issues
The Washington Post	Newspaper	World Power – USA; World Issues
Mail & Guardian	Newspaper	World Power – South Africa
The Rio Times	Newspaper	World Power – Brazil
The Local	News	World Powers – European countries

Key figures or organisations to follow on Twitter

- The current Prime Minister
- The leaders of UK and Scottish political parties
- Your local MSP and MP
- The Scottish Parliament
- The Scottish Prison Service

- The current President of the USA
- The White House
- The United Nations
- The European Union
- The African Union
- Amnesty International

Don't worry if you don't have access to social media, you can keep yourself up to date with news programmes on the television every day as well as local or national newspapers. Your school library should have a selection of newspapers for you to read. Keep an eye on the TV schedule for regular programmes about topics you are studying. These include:

Panorama (BBC1) and **Dispatches** (Channel 4) are documentary series covering current events and issues in the UK and across the world. Their programming may examine issues related to Democracy in Scotland and the UK; Social Inequality; Crime and the Law; World Powers and World Issues.

Question Time (BBC1), **The Politics Show** (BBC1) and **Newsnight** (BBC2) are all programmes in which leaders and members of political parties are invited on to discuss and debate policies. The issues covered will mostly relate to Democracy in Scotland and the UK and Social Inequality.

Remember there may also be one-off programmes or documentaries that could relate to your course. If you miss any relevant programmes on scheduled television you can always watch them using online media such as BBC iPlayer and Channel 4 On Demand.

Using all the suggested media will certainly keep you up to date and will help you put your learning into context. To ensure it is not a wasted effort and you don't forget the information, it is a good idea to take note of **some** of the information you read or watch. This may save you **a lot** of time when you come to research your chosen assignment topic and will certainly aid your revision for the final exam. It is best to keep your notes organised, so use a separate A4 pad or jotter from your class work. Make sure to note:

- date of programme
- the issue or topic the programme is focussed on
- the source of the programme e.g. Channel 4, BBC
- informative and relevant notes about the content of the programme
- any bias or anything the programme failed to mention.

Specialised Modern Studies vocabulary

Throughout your time as a Modern Studies student you will come across new words which will extend your vocabulary. Recognising, understanding and using the specialised vocabulary will help you in your research, revision and exam performance. Some key Modern Studies vocabulary is shown below. Bear in mind this list is not exhaustive and you should try to familiarise yourself with as many as possible. Refer to the Glossary on page 139 for definitions.

Accountable	Exaggeration	Policy
Administration	Executive	Poll
Affiliate	Federal	Prejudice
Alliance	Finance	President
Assimilate	First Minister	Pressure
Asylum	Fiscal	Prime Minister
Austerity	Flagship	Principle
Autonomy	Floating voter	Private sector
Ballot	G20	Privilege
Barnett formula	GDP	Progressive
Benefit	Government	Proportional
Biased	Holyrood	Proposal
Bureaucracy	Ideology	Public sector
Candidate	Immigrant/Immigration	Rebuttal
Census	Inclusion	Recession
Coalition	Inequality	Recommendation
Commission	Influence	Referendum
Committee	Institution	Represent/Representation
Compromise	Intervene/Intervention	Revolutionise
Coup	Left-wing	Right-wing
Consensus	Legislation	Sanction
Constituency	Liberal/Liberalism	Scrutinise/Scrutiny
Council	Majority	Secretary
Democracy	Manifesto	Security
Demographic	Migrant/Migration	Social exclusion
Deploy	Military	Social mobility
Development	Minister	Third sector
Devolution	Minority	Transferable
Devo-max	Nuclear	Transparent
Diplomacy/Diplomatic	Opinion	Treaty
Discrimination	Opposition	Veto
Economic migrant	Parliament	Welfare
Economy	Participation	Westminster
Embargo	Partisan	Working class

The Higher Modern Studies exam paper: knowledge questions

You will have two hours and fifteen minutes to complete the Higher Modern Studies paper. There are a total of 60 marks available in the exam paper. Depending on the topics you have studied (excluding your Assignment) you will complete certain sections of the exam paper. You will be directed to the appropriate section on the front cover of the exam paper as shown in the example below:

Total marks — 60

SECTION 1 — DEMOCRACY IN SCOTLAND AND THE UNITED KINGDOM — 20 marks
Attempt Question 1 and **EITHER** Question 2(a) **OR** 2(b)

SECTION 2 — SOCIAL ISSUES IN THE UNITED KINGDOM — 20 marks
Part A Social inequality in the United Kingdom
Part B Crime and the law in the United Kingdom
Attempt Question 1 and **EITHER** Question 2(a) **OR** 2(b) **OR** 2(c) **OR** 2(d)

SECTION 3 — INTERNATIONAL ISSUES — 20 marks
Part A World powers
Part B World issues
Attempt **EITHER** Question 1(a) **OR** 1(b) **OR** 1(c) **OR** 1(d)

Write your answers clearly in the answer booklet provided. In the answer booklet, you must clearly identify the question number you are attempting.
Use **blue** or **black** ink.

Before leaving the examination room you must give your answer booklet to the Invigilator; if you do not, you may lose all the marks for this paper.

As shown above, each section is worth 20 marks. In Section 1 you will have the option to answer the knowledge-based questions using information about Scotland or the UK or both. This means you can make reference to **Scottish Politics** and the **Scottish Parliament** or **UK Politics** and **Westminster** or both.

For Section 2 – Social Issues in the United Kingdom, you will have studied one of two topics. Either **Social Inequality** in the United Kingdom or **Crime and Law** in the United Kingdom. Again, for the knowledge-based questions you can use information about Scotland or the UK or both in your answers.

In Section 3 you will refer to Part A if you have studied a World Power or Part B if you have studied a World Issue. World Powers include the study of any **G20** country including the **USA**, **China**, **South Africa**, **Brazil** or **Germany**, to name a few. World Issues include the study of a significant and temporary issue affecting the international community. These include **Terrorism**, **Poverty**, **Child Soldiers**, **Nuclear Proliferation**, **Economic Crisis** or the **Effects of War**. Since schools have a vast range of countries and issues to study, the questions in this section will not refer specifically to the country or issue which you have studied. Instead the question will allow for a broad interpretation by learners who will have studied a variety of content for this Unit.

What types of questions will I be asked in the exam?

Example questions for each Unit of study are shown later in this chapter.

Type of question	Skill assessed	Mark allocation	Section of paper	Choice of question to answer
Knowledge and understanding	Analysis **and** evaluation	20	Section 1,2 or 3	Yes
Knowledge and understanding	Analysis **or** evaluation	12	Section 1,2 or 3	Yes
Source-based information handling	Detecting and explaining the degree of objectivity	8	Section 1,2 or 3	No
Source-based information handling	Drawing and supporting complex conclusions	8	Section 1,2 or 3	No

Knowledge and understanding questions

Knowledge and understanding questions are worth a total of **44 marks** of the available 60 in the exam paper – almost three quarters of the total marks. Therefore, it is important you understand how to approach these questions. There are four distinct types of extended responses you are expected to give. The exam paper will ask you four different questions:

1. Discuss...

2. To what extent...

Both are worth **20 marks** each.

3. Analyse...

4. Evaluate...

Both are worth **12 marks** each.

In the exam you will therefore be required to answer the following for a total of 60 marks:

1 x 20-mark question which will either be a Discuss... or To what extent...
1 x 12-mark Analyse question
1 x 12-mark Evaluate question
1 x 8-mark objective source-based question
1 x 8-mark conclusion source-based question

Before we begin to consider how to answer these question stems we must learn the Golden Rules to extended response writing in Modern Studies.

Extended response Golden Rules

✓ Read the question carefully and identify the **skill** and **issue** you need to address
✓ Consider three or four points for a 12-mark response and between four and six points for a 20-mark response
✓ Include relevant and up-to-date examples and evidence – provide one example for every point you make
✓ Balance your answer – analyse and/or evaluate evidence from different points of view
✓ For a 12-mark response, follow instruction and **either** analyse **or** evaluate
✓ For a 20-mark response, analyse, evaluate and structure a line of argument
✓ Draw a valid conclusion and address the question
✓ Never 'turn' the question into another question
✓ Never use out-of-date information from more than 7 years ago

Note: You should only use information older than 7 years if you wish to compare it to modern day to identify a trend or a change.

Modern Studies skills

'The answer is in the question'.

This may seem like a bizarre concept but the question is designed to tell you exactly what you need to do. All that is required from you is to identify this and add in the knowledge you learned in class.

Question	Your instruction
To what extent...?	Consider how much
Discuss	Consider how accurate
Analyse	Examine in detail
Evaluate	Make a judgement about the significance

Do not let the wording of the question put you off. After all, the exam is only testing you on skills you have been practising in all your school subjects for years. These are called higher-order thinking skills. You may recognise the diagram below from your school:

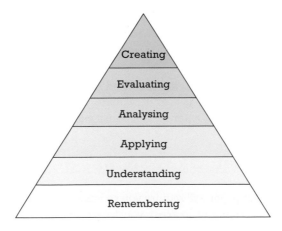

Your role as a Modern Studies student is therefore to **remember** and **understand** the information you are taught as part of the course. You must then **apply** the relevant and appropriate knowledge to the exam question. You must **analyse** and/or **evaluate** the information you have remembered in order to **create** your response.

These same skills will be tested when you complete your assignment report under controlled conditions. You will be asked to apply the research you have remembered and understood and by analysing and evaluating it you will create a report.

The key to success in Higher Modern Studies

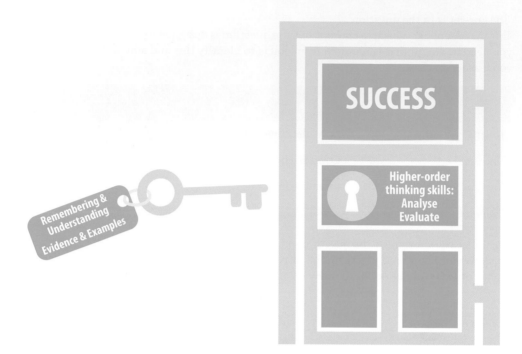

Take the examples and evidence you have learned when studying the course. Use your higher-order thinking skills to analyse and evaluate your examples. This approach will allow you to be successful in your extended response answers.

Examples of 12-mark response questions

The Modern Studies exam paper will require you to answer two types of questions worth 12 marks each. The question will instruct you to either analyse or evaluate an issue. Remember, to **analyse** means you have to **examine something in detail**. If you are asked to **evaluate** you have to **make a judgement**.

Look at the following examples of 12-mark questions. Remember the Golden Rules – the first thing you need to do is identify the **skill** and **issue** you need to address. This will help you determine what you are being instructed to do. Then you must remember three or four points to apply to your answer. Think of what you learned in that particular area of study that is relevant to the question. Look at the examples below to help you understand what the questions are asking you to do and how to plan your written response. Relevant examples are shown in the answers below and are by no means the only answers available. You should refer to the information in your class notes.

Planning and creating an analytical response

Democracy in Scotland and the UK

Q There are many different factors which influence voting behaviour.

Analyse the different factors which affect **voting behaviour**.

You should refer to voting behaviour in Scotland **or** the United Kingdom **or** both in your answer.   **12 marks**

The issue is voting behaviour.

This question is instructing you to examine, in detail, the factors which influence the way people vote.

Points you could include in your answer (choose three or four):

- the media
- social class
- age
- gender
- geography/location

Q Parliamentary representatives carry out different roles as part of the decision making processes of parliament.

Analyse the different **roles** carried out by parliamentary **representatives** in the decision making processes of parliament.

You should refer to parliamentary representatives in Scotland **or** the United Kingdom **or** both in your answer.   **12 marks**

The issue is the work of representatives.

This question is instructing you to examine, in detail, the work representatives do as part of the decision making process.

Points you could include in your answer (choose three or four):

- work in the chamber i.e. debates and voting; Questions to Ministers; Motions
- committee work
- the role of Whips

Social Issues in the United Kingdom: Social Inequality in the United Kingdom

Q Answers may refer to Scotland **or** the UK **or** both.

Analyse government **policies** which aim to reduce **wealth inequalities**.   **12 marks**

The issue is policies to reduce wealth inequalities.

This question is instructing you to examine, in detail, government policies which aim to help poor people.

Points you could include in your answer (choose three or four):

• welfare provision such as housing, education, benefits, healthcare and social services
• changes to the welfare system such as Universal Credit and/or the Bedroom Tax
• income tax threshold
• the national living wage
• Scottish policies such as free personal care

Q Answers may refer to Scotland **or** the UK **or** both.

Analyse the different **lifestyle choices** that may result in **poor health**.   **12 marks**

The issue is the impact of lifestyle on health.

The question is instructing you to examine, in detail, the lifestyle choices which cause poor health.

Points you could include in your answer (choose three or four):

• smoking, diet, alcohol consumption, lack of exercise
• government policies and health initiatives
• official reports and research
• drug misuse
• the increase of sexually transmitted diseases (STDs)
• use of preventative care services

Social Issues in the United Kingdom: Crime and the Law in the United Kingdom

Q Answers may refer to Scotland **or** the UK **or** both.

Analyse the **effects** of crime on society.   **12 marks**

The issue is the effects of crime.

The question is instructing you to examine, in detail, the ways in which crime affects people, communities and/or the economy.

Points you could include in your answer (choose three or four):

- the physical effects of crime i.e. violent crime
- the emotional effects of crime
- the effects of crime on vulnerable groups e.g. children, ethnic minorities, women, the elderly
- the cost of crime for society
- the effects of crime on the offender
- the effects of crime on communities

Q | Answers may refer to Scotland **or** the UK **or** both.

Analyse the government policies which aim to **reduce crime** rates.　　**12 marks**

The issue is reducing crime.

The question is instructing you to examine, in detail, government policies which aim to prevent crime and criminality.

Points you could include in your answer (choose three or four):

- crime investigation
- inclusion
- rehabilitation programmes
- parenting classes

International Issues: Part A: World Powers

Q | With reference to a world power you have studied:

Analyse the government policies which have been introduced to **reduce inequalities**.　　**12 marks**

The issue is inequalities.

The question is instructing you to examine, in detail, government policies which aim to reduce social, economic and/or political inequalities.

World Power: China

Points you could include in your answer (choose three or four):

- development of a socialist market economy
- five-year programme
- policies to reduce rural poverty
- policies to improve health
- policies to curb pollution
- policies to improve education

Q | With reference to a world power you have studied:

Analyse the role this world power takes in **world affairs**.   **12 marks**

The issue is world affairs.

The question is instructing you to examine, in detail, the influence the world power has on international affairs.

World Power: USA

Points you could include in your answer (choose three or four):

- US military intervention abroad
- US involvement in international aid missions
- the US and the UN
- the US and the fight against international terrorism
- the US and international climate change negotiations

International Issues: Part B: World Issues

Q | With reference to a world issue you have studied:

Analyse the **consequences** of a world issue you have studied on those affected.   **12 marks**

The issue is consequences.

This question is instructing you to examine, in detail, the consequences of the world issue on the people affected by it.

World Issue: War and Conflict

Points you could include in your answer (three or four):

- the consequences of the conflict in the Middle East
- the consequences of the conflict in Afghanistan
- the consequences of the conflict in Syria
- the consequences of the conflict in Ukraine
- the consequences of the conflict in Libya

Q With reference to a world issue you have studied:

Analyse the **actions taken by international organisations** to solve an issue. **12 marks**

The issue is international organisations.

This question is instructing you to examine, in detail, what international organisations have done to help the world issue.

Points you could include in your answer (three or four):

- the United Nations and its associated agencies e.g. World Health Programme, Food and Agriculture Organisation, United Nations Children's Fund etc
- NGOs
- the European Union
- the African Union
- the North Atlantic Treaty Organisation
- the World Bank
- the International Monetary Fund

Creating an analytical response

It is a very good idea to write a short, concise introduction of two or three sentences, which sets out what you intend to write about. This will help you gather your thoughts and if you refer back to your introduction it will ensure you remain on track and write what you set out to.

In the main part of your answer the SQA are looking for the following:

SQA principal marking guidelines on 12-mark response state:

- Up to **8 marks** will be awarded for demonstration of a candidate's knowledge and understanding (**KU**) – description, explanation and exemplification.
- Up to **4 marks** awarded for **analytical comments**.
- A **maximum** of **6 marks** can be awarded **per point**.
- Where a candidate makes more analytical points than are required to gain the maximum allocation of 4 marks, these can be credited as KU marks provided they meet the criteria for this.
- An **analysis** mark should be awarded where a candidate uses their knowledge and understanding to identify relevant components (e.g. of an idea, theory, argument etc) and clearly shows at least one of the following:
  - links between different components
  - links between component(s) and the whole
  - links between component(s) and related concepts
  - similarities and contradictions
  - consistency and inconsistency
  - different views/interpretations
  - possible consequences/implications
  - the relative importance of components
  - understanding of underlying order or structure.

This may sound quite complicated, but look at the following example answers to see where marks are awarded. Remember the SQA are looking for you to examine your knowledge in detail so it is important you do not describe the course content. You must also include relevant exemplification. The best way to approach your response is to consider evidence and examples which are relevant to the points you have decided to include, and consider why this is a good example and what it shows in regard to the issue in the question.

To help you construct your extended response consider the following structure for your points:

PEE then Think

Point
Explain
Example
Think (Analysis)

Consider evidence or an example (a piece of legislation/report/ statistic/person) and explain what this shows in relation to the issue in the question.

You do not need to follow the above structure strictly when writing your paragraph, but you should most definitely aim to include each element (Point, Explain, Example and Think). The following example answers will make this clear.

Referring to the example extended response questions we planned out earlier, we shall now construct our answers using the **Point, Explain, Example** and **Think** structure. Look at the examples below:

Example analytical paragraph 1

Q Parliamentary representatives carry out different roles as part of the decision making processes of parliament.

Analyse the different **roles** carried out by parliamentary **representatives** in the decision making processes of parliament.

You should refer to parliamentary representatives in Scotland **or** the United Kingdom **or** both in your answer.   **12 marks**

The issue is the work of representatives.

This question is instructing you to examine, in detail, the work representatives do as part of the decision making process.

One point we could write about in this answer is:

Committee work.

Remember to consider the following structure for your point:

PEE then Think
Point
Explain
Example
Think (Analysis)

Let's think of an example or piece of evidence we know that shows the work of MSPs or MPs in committees.

Higher-order thinking skills: Remember & understand

There are different Scottish Parliament committees with cross-party members such as the Justice Committee. They scrutinise legislation and suggest changes to existing laws.

Now that you have remembered this piece of information think about what this shows in regard to the work MSPs do and use this to construct your **'PEE then Think'** paragraph. Make it clear from the first sentence what the paragraph is going to be about:

Parliamentary representatives, such as MSPs, work in committees as part of the decision making process of parliament. Point Much of the work of the Scottish Parliament is carried out by committees. Explain Membership of the committees reflects the balance of power in the Parliament. [1 KU mark] Example For example, MSPs can be a member of the Justice Committee if they wish. [1 KU mark] Think Committees therefore meet to scrutinise proposed legislation and decide on changes to a law. [1 analysis mark]

This paragraph would score **3 marks**. It contains an accurate point with a short explanation and relevant exemplification. The work of committees has been analysed to an extent in regard to the decision making process. But we could use higher-order thinking skills to handle the point in more depth. Therefore we need to think more about our point and exemplification in reference to the **issue** in the question:

Higher-order thinking skills: Analyse

Fifteen different Scottish Parliament committees with cross-party members such as the Justice Committee – Prisoners (Control of Release) (Scotland) Bill.
They are powerful and affect decisions because they scrutinise legislation and can recommend new laws.

This paragraph is better:

Parliamentary representatives, such as MSPs, work in committees as part of the decision making process of parliament. Point Much of the work of the Scottish Parliament is carried out by committees. Explain There are fifteen committees and cross-party membership reflects the balance of power in the Parliament. [1 KU mark] Committees are an important aspect of an MSP's work since they meet twice a week. MSPs decide which committee they would like to join. [1 KU mark] Example For example, MSPs can be a member of the Justice Committee if they wish, which is currently considering the Prisoners (Control of Release) (Scotland) Bill which aims to end automatic early release for some prisoners. [1 KU mark] Think Committees therefore meet to scrutinise proposed legislation, hear evidence from experts and ask government ministers questions on their particular area of responsibility. [1 KU mark] As such they are sometimes referred to as the 'powerhouse of parliament'. [1 analysis mark] They can also influence decision making by suggesting a new law by putting forward a Committee Bill to parliament, although this does not happen often. [1 analysis mark]

This paragraph would score **6 marks** because it has used relevant exemplification and higher-order thinking skills. The explanation of committees has highlighted to the exam marker that you have understood the point that committees play an important role in parliament. Relevant exemplification has been used to prove this is in fact the case.

The role of committees has therefore been analysed to show one aspect of the decision making process parliamentary representatives are a part of. The role of committees has been examined in detail. This paragraph has successfully:

> ✓ included information relevant to the issue and explained this well
> ✓ included relevant and up-to-date examples and evidence – no more than 7 years old
> ✓ analysed the information and example by examining it in detail
> ✓ followed instruction from the question by remembering appropriate information and analysing it

Example analytical paragraph 2

Q Answers may refer to Scotland **or** the UK **or** both.

Analyse the different **lifestyle** choices that may result in **poor health**.   **12 marks**

The issue is the effects of lifestyle on health.

This question is instructing you to examine, in detail, the lifestyle choices which cause poor health.

One point we could write about in this answer is:

Alcohol consumption.

Remember to consider the following structure for your points:

PEE then Think
Point
Explain
Example
Think (Analysis)

Let's think of an example or piece of evidence we know that shows alcohol can cause poor health.

Higher-order thinking skills: Remember & understand

Deaths from alcohol-related liver disease have risen.

Now that you have remembered this piece of information think about what this shows in regard to poor health and use this to construct your **'PEE then Think'** paragraph. Make it clear from the first sentence what the paragraph is going to be about:

Point Alcohol consumption is a lifestyle choice that may result in poor health. Explain Too much consumption of alcohol can affect behaviour and physical health. It can cause liver disease. [1 KU mark] *Example Death rates linked to alcohol-related liver disease have risen considerably over the last few decades and alcohol is now one of the most common causes of death in the UK.* [1 KU mark] *Think Alcohol is a lifestyle choice that damages health and if people choose to binge drink they can cause long-term damage to their bodies.* [1 analysis mark]

This paragraph would score **3 marks**. It contains an accurate point with a short explanation and relevant exemplification. The effects of alcohol on health has been analysed to an extent, but we could use higher-order thinking skills to handle the point in more depth. Therefore, we need to think more about our point and exemplification in reference to the **issue** in the question:

Higher-order thinking skills: Analyse

Deaths from alcohol-related liver disease have risen. Research also shows more professionals and those over 65 are consuming too much alcohol. Minimum price on alcohol.

This paragraph is better:

Point Alcohol consumption is a lifestyle choice that may result in poor health. Explain Too much consumption of alcohol over a long period of time can result in serious health implications. It can cause liver disease. [1 KU mark] *Example Death rates linked to alcohol-related liver disease have risen considerably over the last few decades and alcohol is now one of the most common causes of death in the UK.* [1 KU mark] *Think Alcohol is a lifestyle choice that is worryingly embedded in British binge-drinking culture.* [1 analysis mark] *Furthermore, research shows more young professionals are drinking over the recommended amount in a bid to cope with work stress. Also more over 65s are consuming too much which could be a result of retirement and social gatherings or self-medicating to cope with loneliness.* [1 analysis mark] *The Scottish government has attempted to curb the Scottish drinking culture since Scotland has a higher rate of alcohol-related deaths than anywhere else in the UK.* [1 KU mark] *The Scottish government have passed a bill to introduce a minimum price on alcohol in the hope that people will consume less because it costs more when the policy is introduced.* [1 analysis mark]

This paragraph would score **6 marks** because it has used relevant exemplification and higher-order thinking skills. The explanation has highlighted the link to poor health. Relevant exemplification has been used to prove the detrimental effect of alcohol consumption. The impact of alcohol on health has therefore been analysed to show examples of groups of society who make this lifestyle choice and attempts to reduce alcohol consumption. The impact of alcohol on health has been examined in detail. This paragraph has successfully:

> ✓ included information relevant to the issue and explained this well
> ✓ included relevant and up-to-date examples and evidence – no more than 7 years old
> ✓ analysed the information and example by examining it in detail
> ✓ followed instruction from the question by remembering appropriate information and analysing it

Example analytical paragraph 3

Q Answers may refer to Scotland **or** the UK **or** both.

Analyse the **effects** of **crime** on society.   **12 marks**

The issue is the effects of crime.

This question is instructing you to examine, in detail, the ways in which crime affects people, communities and/or the economy.

One point we could write about in this answer is:

The emotional effects of crime on the victims.

Remember to consider the following structure for your points:

PEE then Think
Point
Explain
Example
Think (Analysis)

Let's think of an example or piece of evidence we know that shows the emotional effects of crime.

> **Higher-order thinking skills: Remember & understand**
>
> Murder can be very traumatic and cause emotional and practical problems. The largest survey of families affected by murder showed over 80% suffered trauma-related symptoms.

Now that you have remembered this piece of information think about what this shows in regard to poor health and use this to construct your **'PEE then Think'** paragraph. Make it clear from the first sentence what the paragraph is going to be about:

Point The emotional impact of crime on victims and families can be devastating. Explain Murder is the most serious crime which affects not only the victims but families and communities. [1 KU mark] Example In 2011 research was carried out by the Commissioner for Victims and Witnesses involving 400 families affected by homicide. The results showed over 80% suffered trauma-related symptoms. [1 KU mark] Think The emotional strain of their loss can cause depression, anxiety and feelings of guilt, as well as physical consequences such as high blood pressure. [1 analysis mark]

This paragraph would score **3 marks**. It contains an accurate point with a short explanation and relevant exemplification. The emotional effects of murder on victims' families has been analysed to an extent, but we need to use higher-order thinking skills to handle the point in more depth. Therefore, we could think more about our point and exemplification in reference to the **issue** in the question:

Higher-order thinking skills: Analyse

Murder can be very traumatic and cause emotional and practical problems. The largest survey of families affected by murder showed over 80% suffered trauma-related symptoms. The results can cause job losses, create custody issues and re-schooling.

This paragraph is better:

Point The emotional impact of crime on victims and families can be devastating. Explain Murder is the most serious crime which affects not only the victims but families and communities for many years. [1 KU mark] Those who knew the victim must deal with their own bereavement as well as a police investigation and court case. [1 KU mark] Example In 2011 research was carried out by the Commissioner for Victims and Witnesses, the largest survey to date involved 400 families affected by homicide. The results showed over 80% suffered trauma-related symptoms. [1 KU mark] Think The emotional strain of their loss can cause depression, anxiety and feelings of guilt, as well as physical consequences such as high blood pressure. This can lead to extended sick leave and/ or redundancy on the grounds of ill-health which can also have financial implications for the family. This will create additional stress. [2 analysis marks] Grandparents may take on responsibility for children following the death of a parent which can be further complicated when one parent has killed the other. Families may have to move to escape the memories of the murder if it has taken place in or near the home. This means children may also have to move to a new school. [2 analysis marks] Families affected by murder can experience a range of long-lasting emotional trauma.

This paragraph would score the maximum **6 marks** available because it has used relevant exemplification and higher-order thinking skills. The explanation has highlighted the on-going complex nature of murder cases. Relevant exemplification has been used to show the available statistical evidence. The emotional effects of murder on the victim's family have then been examined in detailed. This paragraph has successfully:

✓ included information relevant to the issue and explained this well
✓ included relevant and up-to-date examples and evidence – no more than 7 years old
✓ analysed the information and example by examining it in detail
✓ followed instruction from the question by remembering appropriate information and analysing it

Example analytical paragraph 4

Q With reference to a world power you have studied:

Analyse the government policies which have been introduced to **reduce inequalities.**

12 marks

The issue is inequalities.

This question is instructing you to examine, in detail, government policies to reduce social, economic and/or political inequalities.

World Power: China

One point we could write about in this answer is:

Policies to improve health: Healthy China 2020.

Remember to consider the following structure for your points:

PEE then Think
Point
Explain
Example
Think (Analysis)

Let's think of an example or piece of evidence we know that shows policies to improve health.

Now that you have remembered this piece of information think about what this shows in regard to poor health and use this to construct your **'PEE then Think'** paragraph. Make it clear from the first sentence what the paragraph is going to be about:

Point A government policy which aims to reduce health inequalities in China is Healthy China 2020. Explain This programme aims to provide essential primary healthcare services for all in China and provide more insurance coverage for people. [1 KU mark] *Example There has been progress in the last 10 years with more than one billion people with insurance coverage and an additional one million doctors.* [1 KU mark] *Think Therefore, the Healthy China 2020 programme is making progress in reducing health inequalities especially amongst the vulnerable migrant workers, many of whom do not have or do not know if they have health insurance.* [1 analysis mark]

This paragraph would score **3 marks**. It contains an accurate point with a short explanation and relevant exemplification. The policy has been analysed to an extent, but we could use higher-order thinking skills to handle the point in more depth. Therefore, we need to think more about our point and exemplification in reference to the **issue** in the question:

This paragraph is better:

Point A government policy which aims to reduce health inequalities in China is Healthy China 2020. Explain This programme aims to provide essential primary healthcare services for all in China and provide more insurance coverage for people. Many migrant workers, due to the nature of their employment, do not know if they have coverage and therefore many struggle with poverty from expensive healthcare bills. [2 KU marks] *Example There has been progress in the last 10 years with over one billion more people with insurance coverage and an additional one million doctors.* [1 KU mark] *Think Therefore, the Healthy China 2020 programme is making progress in reducing health inequalities especially amongst the vulnerable migrant workers, but much more work is needed especially in regard to reforming hospital funding. A toxic patient-doctor relationship exists since many doctors are paid per service by their hospital. The government must convince hospitals to change this model to ensure patients trust their health professionals when seeking medical assistance. Considerable improvements have been made in the fine-tuning of health insurance programmes, but more work is needed to reduce health inequalities.* [3 analysis marks]

This paragraph would score **6 marks** because it has used relevant exemplification and higher-order thinking skills. The explanation has highlighted successes of the policy. The exemplification has been put into context and further analysed in relation to the issue in the question. This paragraph has successfully:

> ✓ included information relevant to the issue and explained this well
> ✓ included relevant and up-to-date examples and evidence – no more than 7 years old
> ✓ analysed the information and example by examining it in detail
> ✓ followed instruction from the question by remembering appropriate information and analysing it

Example analytical paragraph 5

Q **Analyse** the **consequences** of a world issue you have studied on those affected.

12 marks

The issue is consequences.

This question is instructing you to examine, in detail, the consequences of the world issue on the people affected by it.

World Issue: War and Conflict

One point we could write about in this answer is:

The consequences of the conflict in Ukraine.

Remember to consider the following structure for your points:

PEE then Think
Point
Explain
Example
Think (Analysis)

Let's think of an example or piece of evidence we know that shows the consequences of the conflict in Ukraine.

Now that you have remembered this piece of information think about what this shows in regard to poor health and use this to construct your **'PEE then Think'** paragraph. Make it clear from the first sentence what the paragraph is going to be about:

Point Ukraine was once part of the Soviet Union but Russian President Vladimir Putin annexed Crimea in 2014. Explain The Russian people and pro-Russians in Ukraine have been told that Crimea is simply returning to the motherland. [1 KU mark] *Example Yet over 4000 citizens and soldiers have died in the conflict.* [1 KU mark] *Think This shows that not all Ukrainians feel that the return of Crimea to Russian control is a good thing and the people of Crimea have effectively lost their Ukrainian nationality.* [1 analysis mark]

This paragraph would score **3 marks**. It contains an accurate point with a short explanation and relevant exemplification. The effect on the people of Crimea has been analysed to an extent, but we could use higher-order thinking skills to handle the point in more depth.

Therefore we need to think more about our point and exemplification in reference to the **issue** in the question:

This paragraph is better:

Point Ukraine was once part of the Soviet Union but Russian President Vladimir Putin annexed Crimea in 2014. Explain The Russian people and pro-Russians in Ukraine have been told that Crimea is simply returning to the motherland. The media is controlled by the Russian government and many people therefore believe that the Ukrainian government is persecuting pro-Russians in Ukraine. [2 KU marks] *Example Over 4000 citizens and soldiers have died in the conflict and economic sanctions have been imposed by the West to show their disapproval of the annexation.* [1 KU mark] *Think However not all Ukrainians feel that the return of Crimea to Russian control is a good thing and the people of Crimea have effectively lost their Ukrainian nationality. The economic sanctions have had an impact too as the Russian currency has lost value and businesses have suffered.* [2 analysis marks] *Furthermore, the Crimean authorities have severely limited the amount people can withdraw from their savings. Therefore, the people in Ukraine have suffered economically and many have had to flee the fighting.* [2 analysis marks]

This paragraph would score the maximum **6 marks** available because it has used relevant exemplification and higher-order thinking skills. The explanation has shown the extent to which the Russian government is controlling the situation and the impact this has had on the people. The exemplification has been put into context and further analysed in relation to the issue in the question. This paragraph has successfully:

> ✓   included information relevant to the issue and explained this well
> ✓   included relevant and up-to-date examples and evidence – no more than 7 years old
> ✓   analysed the information and example by examining it in detail
> ✓   followed instruction from the question by remembering appropriate information and analysing it

Planning and creating an evaluative response

Democracy in Scotland and the United Kingdom

Q The leader of the government is important in decision making.

Evaluate the importance of the leader of the government in **decision making**.

You should refer to the leader of the government in Scotland **or** the United Kingdom **or** both in your answer. **12 marks**

The issue is decision making.

This question is instructing you to make a judgement about decision making in government.

Points you could include in your answer (choose three or four):

- the role of the Prime Minister/First Minister in decision making
- the role of backbenchers/other MSPs in decision making
- the role of committees in decision making
- the role of the House of Lords in decision making

Q Short-term factors are important in influencing voter behaviour.

Evaluate the importance of **short-term factors** in influencing voting behaviour.

You should refer to voting behaviour in Scotland **or** the United Kingdom **or** both in your answer. **12 marks**

The issues are short-term voting factors.

This question is instructing you to make a judgement about the various short-term factors which influence voting behaviour.

Points you could include in your answer (choose three or four):

- media – newspapers, TV debates, social media
- leadership style
- election campaign and party image
- party policies – single-issue voting

Social Issues in the United Kingdom: Social Inequality in the United Kingdom

Q Answers may refer to Scotland **or** the UK **or** both.

Evaluate the main causes of **social inequality** in society.   **12 marks**

The issue is social inequality.

This question is instructing you to make a judgement about the main causes of social inequality.

Points you could include in your answer (choose three or four):

- poverty and deprivation
- lifestyle choices
- government policies
- discrimination
- lack of social mobility
- collectivist and individualist perspectives

Q Answers may refer to Scotland **or** the UK **or** both.

Evaluate the impact of **government policies** in tackling **social inequalities. 12 marks**

The issue is government policies in relation to social inequality.

This question is instructing you to make a judgement about the impact government policies have on inequalities.

Points you could include in your answer (choose three or four):

- the Equality Act
- the National Living Wage
- free prescriptions in Scotland
- university tuition fees
- free school meals (P1-3)
- minimum pricing

Social Issues in the United Kingdom: Crime and the Law in the United Kingdom

Q Answers may refer to Scotland **or** the UK **or** both.

Evaluate the view that crime only **affects the victims**.   **12 marks**

The issue is the effect of crime.

This question is instructing you to make a judgement about the effects of crime.

Points you could include in your answer (choose three or four):

- the impact crime has on the victim – physically, mentally and emotionally
- the impact crime has on the community
- the impact crime has on the economy

Q Answers may refer to Scotland **or** the UK **or** both.

Evaluate different **policies** which aim to **reduce reoffending** rates.　　**12 marks**

The issue is reducing reoffending.

This question is instructing you to make a judgement about the policies designed to reduce reoffending.

Points you could include in your answer (choose three or four):

- alternatives to prison such as Community Payback Orders; Restriction of Liberty Orders; Drug Treatment and Testing Orders; Anti-social Behaviour Orders; probation
- restorative justice

International Issues: Part A: World Powers

Q With reference to a world power you have studied:

Evaluate the ways **citizens** are able to **influence the political system**.　　**12 marks**

The issue is the influence of citizens on politics.

This question is instructing you to make a judgement about the influence citizens can have on politics in the country you studied.

Points you could include in your answer (choose three or four):

- voter participation and turnout – elections/referendums/propositions
- disenfranchisement
- membership and influence of pressure groups/interest groups
- recent protests
- freedom of speech and use of social media

Q With reference to a world power you have studied:

Evaluate the effectiveness of **government policies to reduce social and economic inequalities**.   **12 marks**

The issue is government policies to reduce social and economic inequalities.

This question is instructing you to make a judgement about whether the policies have improved social and economic inequalities.

Points you could include in your answer (choose three or four):

• government policies to improve social inequalities such as housing, education, health and crime
• government policies to improve economic inequalities such as poverty, income, unemployment

Note: the question specifically states social **and** economic inequalities, therefore your answer cannot be about only social inequalities or only economic inequalities. **Both** social and economic inequalities **must** be included in your answer.

Q With reference to a world power you have studied:

Evaluate whether the political system is **democratic**.   **12 marks**

The issue is democracy.

This question is instructing you to make a judgement about whether the political system is designed to ensure the country is democratic.

World Power: South Africa

Points you could include in your answer (choose three or four):

• the Bill of Rights
• the electoral system and voter choice
• the power of the ANC
• the media

International Issues: Part B: World Issues

Q With reference to a world issue you have studied:

Evaluate the **impact** this issue has had on **different countries**.   **12 marks**

The issue is the impact on different countries.

This question is instructing you to make a judgement about the impact of the issue on different countries.

World Issue: Terrorism

Points you could include in your answer (choose three or four):

- the impact of terrorism in the UK/Europe (ISIS, Al Qaeda, IRA)
- the impact of terrorism in Nigeria (Boko Haram)
- the impact of terrorism in the Middle East (ISIS)
- the impact of terrorism in international relations (UN)

Q With reference to a world issue you have studied:

Evaluate the ways the issue has been **caused by political problems**.   **12 marks**

The issue is the cause of the world issue.

This question is instructing you to make a judgement about whether the issue has only been caused by political issues.

Points you could include in your answer (choose three or four):

- political causes of the world issue
- economic causes of the world issue
- social causes of the world issue
- biological causes of the world issue

Planning and creating an evaluative response

It is a very good idea to write a short, concise introduction which sets out what you intend to write about. This will help you gather your thoughts and if you refer back to your introduction it will ensure you remain on track and write what you set out to.

In the main part of your answer the SQA are looking for the following:

SQA principal marking guidelines on 12-mark responses state:

- Up to **8 marks** will be awarded for demonstration of a candidate's knowledge and understanding (**KU**) – description, explanation and exemplification.
- Up to **4 marks** awarded for **evaluative comments**.
- A **maximum** of **6 marks** can be awarded **per point**.
- Where a candidate makes more evaluative points than are required to gain the maximum allocation of 4 marks, these can be credited as KU marks provided they meet the criteria for this.
- **Evaluation** involves making a judgement(s) based on criteria, drawing conclusions on the extent to which a view is supported by the evidence; counter-arguments including possible alternative interpretations; the overall impact/significance of the factors when taken together; the relative importance of factors in relation to the context.

The SQA are therefore looking for you to make a judgement about your knowledge on an issue, so it is important you do not describe the course content. You must also include relevant exemplification. The best way to approach your response is to consider evidence and examples which are relevant to the points you have decided to include, and consider why this is a good example and what it shows in regard to the issue in the question.

To help you construct your extended response consider the following structure for your points:

PEE then Think
Point
Explain
Example
Think and **Link** (Evaluation)

Consider evidence or an example (a piece of legislation/report/statistic/person) and explain what this shows in relation to the issue in the question.

You do not need to follow the above structure strictly when writing your paragraph, but you should most definitely aim to include each element (Point, Explain, Example, Think and Link). The following example answers will make this clear.

Referring to the example extended response questions we planned out earlier, we shall now construct our answers using the Point, Explain, Example, Think and Link structure. Look at the examples below:

Example evaluative paragraph 1

Q The leader of the government is important in decision making.

Evaluate the importance of the leader of the government in **decision making**.

You should refer to the leader of the government in Scotland **or** the United Kingdom **or** both in your answer. **12 marks**

The issue is decision making.

One point we could write about in this answer is:

The role of the First Minister in decision making.

Remember to consider the following structure for your point:

PEE then Think
Point
Explain
Example
Think and **Link** (Evaluation)

Let's think of an example or piece of evidence we know that shows the role of the First Minister in decision making.

Higher-order thinking skills: Remember & understand

The then First Minister (FM), Alex Salmond, supported the decision to release Lockerbie bomber Al-Megrahi.

Now that you have remembered this piece of information, think about what this shows in regard to the importance of the FM and use this to construct your **'PEE then Think and Link'** paragraph. Make it clear from the first sentence what the paragraph is going to be about:

The First Minister (FM) of Scotland has a significant role as leader of the government. Point Much of the work of the FM requires important decision making. Explain The FM is leader of their party and of the government and can make some very controversial decisions at times. [1 KU mark] Example For example, the former FM, Alex Salmond, supported the decision to release Lockerbie bomber Al-Megrahi from prison and return him to his home country of Libya. [1 KU mark] Think and Link This was not a popular decision and received worldwide media attention, but Alex Salmond upheld this decision and Al-Megrahi did not return to Scotland. This therefore shows that the FM as leader of the government in Scotland is very important in decision making. [1 evaluation mark]

This paragraph would score **3 marks**. It contains an accurate point with a short explanation and relevant exemplification. A weak judgement has been made about the importance of the FM in decision making, but we could use higher-order thinking skills to make this judgement clearer. Therefore, we need to think more about our point and exemplification in reference to the **issue** in the question:

Higher-order thinking skills: Evaluate

The decision to release the Lockerbie bomber was initially made by the Justice Secretary and attracted much criticism from the UK and US governments.

This paragraph is better:

The First Minister (FM) of Scotland has a significant role as leader of the government. Point *Much of the work of the FM requires important decision making.* Explain *The FM is leader of their party and of the government and can make some very controversial decisions at times.* [1 KU mark] Example *For example, the then FM, Alex Salmond, supported the decision by his then Justice Secretary Kenny McAskill to release Lockerbie bomber Al-Megrahi from prison and return him to his home country of Libya on medical grounds.* [1 KU mark] Think and Link *This was not a popular decision and received worldwide media attention. The UK Prime Minister and US President both publicly announced their disapproval of this decision. Despite this, the FM did not back down and upheld this decision as it is well within his powers to do so as the leader of the Scottish government.* [2 KU marks] *In this instance this shows the FM is significantly important in the decision making of government since he personally defended this decision to Parliament, the media and other world leaders.* [1 evaluation mark] *He therefore took responsibility for the actions of his Justice Minister.* [1 evaluation mark]

This paragraph would score **6 marks** because it has used relevant exemplification and higher-order thinking skills. The explanation of the Al-Megrahi case shows the exam marker that you have understood the point that the FM can personally make controversial decisions. Relevant exemplification has been used to prove this is in fact the case. The exemplification has been examined in detail to show its controversy and concluded with the judgement that the First Minister therefore has significant powers in decision making. This paragraph has successfully:

✓   included information relevant to the issue and explained this well
✓   included relevant and up-to-date examples and evidence – no more than 7 years old
✓   evaluated the information and example by making a judgement in reference to the question
✓   followed instruction from the question by remembering appropriate information and making a clear decision

Once the other points have been considered using the Point, Explain, Example, Think and Link structure, a short, concise conclusion will also allow you to be awarded evaluation marks. However, remember not to repeat points you have previously made in your answer. Consider the question in its entirety.

A short evaluative conclusion for this question could be:

As leader of the Scottish government, the First Minister is significantly important in decision making. The First Minister is the public face of government and therefore defends policy ideas and decisions made by his Ministers no matter how controversial they may be. However, in a democratic system these decisions can be scrutinised by others including MSPs in the debating chamber and cross-party committees. The importance of the First Minister in decision making is made less so by the fact that the FM is held accountable to the rest of Parliament.

This paragraph would be awarded 2 evaluative marks. It is concise and sums up the entire answer in relation to the question.

Example evaluative paragraph 2

Q Answers may refer to Scotland **or** the UK **or** both.

Evaluate the impact of **government policies** in tackling **social inequalities**.

12 marks

The issue is government policies in relation to social inequality.

One point we could write about in this answer is:

Free prescriptions.

Remember to consider the following structure for your point:

PEE then Think
Point
Explain
Example
Think and **Link** (Evaluation)

Let's think of an example or piece of evidence about government policies to reduce inequalities.

Higher-order thinking skills: Remember & understand

Prescriptions are free in Scotland compared to £8.40 in England.*

*As at time of print.

Now that you have remembered this piece of information, think about what this shows in regard to social inequality and use this to construct your **'PEE then Think and Link'** paragraph. Make it clear from the first sentence what the paragraph is going to be about:

Point The SNP's flagship policy of free prescription charges was introduced in Scotland in 2011. Explain The policy was aimed at reducing health inequalities by removing the financial barrier for many patients who were left to decide which medications they could afford. [1 KU mark] *Example For example, the cost of prescriptions has risen to £8.40 in England.* [1 KU mark] *Think and Link This policy has been of benefit to non-exempt patients with long-term conditions such as low blood pressure and Parkinsons, and has therefore helped to reduce health inequalities.* [1 evaluation mark]

This paragraph would score **3 marks** because it has used relevant exemplification and higher-order thinking skills. The policy of free prescription charges has been explained and an appropriate example regarding the cost of prescriptions elsewhere in the UK has been used. However, the evaluation is weak and could be expanded. We could use higher-order thinking skills to make the judgement clearer. Therefore, we need to think more about our point and exemplification in reference to the **issue** in the question:

Higher-order thinking skills: Evaluate

The policy has been criticised. It has cost over £900 million so far.*

*As at time of print.

This paragraph is better:

Point The SNP's flagship policy of free prescription charges was introduced in Scotland in 2011. Explain The policy was aimed at reducing health inequalities by removing the financial barrier for many patients who were left to decide which medications they could afford. [1 KU mark] *Example For example, the cost of prescriptions has risen to £8.40 in England.* [1 KU mark] *Think and Link This policy has been of benefit to non-exempt patients with long-term conditions such as low blood pressure and Parkinsons, and has therefore helped to reduce health inequalities.* [1 evaluation mark] *But evidence of the impact of health inequalities can be questioned. The number of prescribed medications has increased year on year so more people are getting medication on the NHS bill instead of buying over the counter.* [1 evaluation mark] *This policy has therefore proved to be expensive at a cost of over £900 million so far which many, including the Scottish Conservatives, would argue could be better spent on other health priorities such as staffing or obesity.* [2 evaluation marks]

This paragraph would score **6 marks** because it has used relevant exemplification and higher-order thinking skills. The policy has been explained and further exemplification has been used to criticise it. Therefore, both sides of the argument have been provided and a judgement has been made. This paragraph has successfully:

✓ included information relevant to the issue and explained this well
✓ included relevant and up-to-date examples and evidence – no more than 7 years old
✓ evaluated the information and example by making a judgement in reference to the question
✓ followed instruction from the question by remembering appropriate information and making a clear decision

Once the other points have been considered using the Point, Explain, Example, Think and Link structure, a short, concise conclusion will also allow you to be awarded evaluation marks. However, remember not to repeat points you have previously made in your answer. Consider the question in its entirety.

A short evaluative conclusion for this question could be:

Government policies to reduce social inequalities have made a difference in some aspects, but generally they do not go far enough to eradicate inequalities. Despite the National Minimum Wage and the Equality Act many still experience in-work poverty and discrimination. There is little evidence to suggest free prescriptions have reduced health inequalities but they have successfully removed the financial barriers associated with ill-health. Similarly, financial barriers have been lifted for tuition fees which makes social mobility more of a possibility for Scottish students.

This paragraph would be awarded 2 evaluative marks. It is concise and sums up the entire answer in relation to the question.

Example evaluative paragraph 3

Q   Answers may refer to Scotland **or** the UK **or** both.

Evaluate different **policies** which aim to **reduce reoffending** rates.   **12 marks**

The issue is reducing reoffending.

One point we could write about in this answer is:

Community Payback Orders.

Remember to consider the following structure for your point:

PEE then Think
Point
Explain
Example
Think and **Link** (Evaluation)

Let's think of an example or piece of evidence we know about Community Payback Orders.

Higher-order thinking skills: Remember & understand

In a 2013 Prison Reform Trust survey of nearly 3000 people on Community Orders, 77% agreed that the Community Order made them less likely to commit crime, and 64% agreed that it had given them an opportunity to give something back to society.

Now that you have remembered this piece of information, think about what this shows in regard to reducing reoffending and use this to construct your **'PEE then Think and Link'** paragraph. Make it clear from the first sentence what the paragraph is going to be about:

Point In an attempt to reduce reoffending one alternative to custodial sentencing is a Community Payback Order. Explain A Community Payback Order requires the offender to carry out unpaid work to benefit the community up to a maximum of 300 hours. They work as part of a team to do things such as clean graffiti or repair local community centres. [1 KU mark] Example In a 2013 Prison Reform Trust survey of nearly 3000 people on Community Orders, 77% agreed that the Community Order made them less likely to commit crime, and 64% agreed that it had given them an opportunity to give something back to society. [1 KU mark] Think and Link Evidently there is some success in reducing reoffending rates with Community Payback Orders. [1 evaluation mark]

This paragraph would score **3 marks** because it has used relevant exemplification and higher-order thinking skills. Community Payback Orders have been explained and an appropriate example regarding reoffending has been used. However, the evaluation is weak and could be expanded:

Higher-order thinking skills: Evaluate

One quarter of offenders may reoffend. Therefore reoffending rates remain. Alternative sentencing does not address the complex causes of crime.

This paragraph is better:

Point In an attempt to reduce reoffending one alternative to custodial sentencing is a community Payback Order. Explain A Community Payback Order requires the offender to carry out unpaid work to benefit the community up to a maximum of 300 hours. They work as part of a team to do things such as clean graffiti or repair local community centres. [1 KU mark] Example In a 2013 Prison Reform Trust survey of nearly 3000 people on Community Orders, 77% agreed that the Community Order made them less likely to commit crime, and 64% agreed that it had given them an opportunity to give something back to society. [1 KU mark] Think and Link Evidently there is some success in reducing reoffending rates with Community Payback Orders since the majority of those serving this sentence think they won't commit crime again. But evidence shows that although they could be deemed a success, there are still almost a quarter of offenders who may consider reoffending. [2 evaluation marks] Community Payback Orders are not a suitable sentence for all crimes and will therefore not reduce reoffending rates on their own. This alternative sentence will not address the complex causes of crime which result in many reoffending, such as addiction issues. [2 evaluation marks]

This paragraph would score **6 marks** because it has used relevant exemplification and higher-order thinking skills. Community Payback Orders have been explained and an appropriate example regarding reoffending has been used. The evaluation has been expanded and clarified. A drawback of the sentence has been given. By stating that this sentence is not suitable for all crimes leads the answers into the next paragraph, which will evaluate another sentence. This paragraph has successfully:

✓   included information relevant to the issue and explained this well
✓   included relevant and up-to-date examples and evidence – no more than 7 years old
✓   evaluated the information and example by making a judgement in reference to the question
✓   followed instruction from the question by remembering appropriate information and making a clear decision

Once the other points have been considered using the Point, Explain, Example, Think and Link structure, a short, concise conclusion will also allow you to be awarded evaluation marks. However, remember not to repeat points you have previously made in your answer.

A short evaluative conclusion for this question could be:

Several different policies are in use in reducing reoffending. No one particular policy will eradicate reoffending altogether. Consideration must be given to each individual case and offender. The causes of crime are complex which also makes reoffending complex. However, alternatives to prison can help reduce reoffending and all have a degree of success which is important to avoid the revolving door of prison.

This paragraph would score 2 evaluative marks. It has considered the issue of reoffending in its entirety while stating the limited success of each alternative to prison considered in the answer.

Example evaluative paragraph 4

Q With reference to a world power you have studied:

Evaluate the ways **citizens** are able to **influence the political system**.   **12 marks**

The issue is the influence of citizens on politics.

World Power: Brazil

One point we could write about in this answer is:

Voter participation and turnout.

Remember to consider the following structure for your point:

PEE then Think
Point
Explain
Example
Think and **Link** (Evaluation)

Let's think of an example or piece of evidence we know about voter participation and turnout in Brazil.

Higher-order thinking skills: Remember & understand

Voter turnout in the 2014 elections was 80% for
Parliamentary elections and 78% for the Presidential election.

Now that you have remembered this piece of information, think about what this shows in regard to the influence of citizens on politics and use this to construct your **'PEE then Think and Link'** paragraph. Make it clear from the first sentence what the paragraph is going to be about:

Point One way in which citizens of Brazil are able to influence the political system is by voting. Explain Brazil has a system of compulsory voting in operation, therefore the turnout at elections is high in order to avoid a fine. [1 KU mark] *Example For example, voter turnout in the recent 2014 elections was 80% for Parliamentary elections and 78% for the Presidential election.* [1 KU mark] *Think and Link This high turnout therefore shows that the citizens of Brazil clearly have an influence on the political system since so many use their democratic right and participate in the make-up of government.* [1 evaluation mark]

This paragraph would score **3 marks** because it has used relevant exemplification and higher-order thinking skills. Voter turnout has been explained and an appropriate example regarding reoffending has been used. However the evaluation is weak and could be expanded:

Higher-order thinking skills: Evaluate

In the 2014 elections almost 20% of the votes were invalid and therefore ineffective.

This paragraph is better:

Point One way in which citizens of Brazil are able to influence the political system is by voting. Explain Brazil has a system of compulsory voting in operation, therefore the turnout at elections is high in order to avoid a fine. [1 KU mark] Example For example, voter turnout in the recent 2014 elections was 80% for Parliamentary elections and 78% for the Presidential election. [1 KU mark] Think and Link This high turnout therefore shows that the citizens of Brazil clearly have an influence on the political system since so many use their democratic right and participate in the make-up of government. [1 evaluation mark] However, a system of compulsory voting can be criticised in that it doesn't necessarily mean that Brazilians are actively participating in the political process and therefore influencing it. [1 evaluation mark] In the 2014 elections almost 20% of the votes were invalid. [1 KU mark] Therefore, a voter may simply turn up to avoid a fine but choose to invalidate their vote or vote with little knowledge. But voting is still an indication of the electorate's wishes and does influence the political system by electing representatives. [1 evaluation mark]

This paragraph would score **6 marks** because it has used relevant exemplification and higher-order thinking skills. It has evaluated the impact of voter turnout, but balanced this by examining another piece of evidence. This is then put into the context of the question and a final judgement is made. This paragraph has successfully:

- ✓ included information relevant to the issue and explained this well
- ✓ included relevant and up-to-date examples and evidence – no more than 7 years old
- ✓ evaluated the information and example by making a judgement in reference to the question
- ✓ followed instruction from the question by remembering appropriate information and making a clear decision

Once the other points have been considered using the Point, Explain, Example, Think and Link structure, a short, concise conclusion will also allow you to be awarded evaluation marks. However, remember not to repeat points you have previously made in your answer.

A short evaluative conclusion for this question could be:

Citizens can influence the political system in Brazil in many ways. Compulsory voting means the turnout at elections is high and therefore the vast majority of the public will express their preferred choice. But not all will vote with an informed choice and prisoners are exempt from voting while in prison. However, Brazil's recent Internet Bill of Rights Law in 2014 and impeachment of President Dilma Rouseff in 2016 show that with the power of petition and protest, Brazil's citizens are significantly influencing government and law making in their country.

This paragraph would score 2 evaluative marks. It has summed up the issues of voting, disenfranchisement, protest and petition and made a judgement about the extent citizens influence the political system.

Example evaluative paragraph 5

> **Q** With reference to a world issue you have studied:
>
> **Evaluate** the **impact** this issue has had on **different countries**.   **12 marks**

The issue is the impact on different countries.

World Issue: Terrorism

One point we could write about in this answer is:

The impact of terrorism in Nigeria (Boko Haram).

Remember to consider the following structure for your point:

PEE then Think
Point
Explain
Example
Think and **Link** (Evaluation)

Let's think of an example or piece of evidence we know that shows the impact of Boko Haram on Nigeria:

Higher-order thinking skills: Remember & understand

Boko Haram kidnapped 276 girls in April 2014.

Now that you have remembered this piece of information, think about what this shows in regard to the impact of terrorism on Nigeria and use this to construct your **'PEE then Think and Link'** paragraph. Make it clear from the first sentence what the paragraph is going to be about:

Point In a bid to create a separate Islamic state, Boko Haram have caused havoc in Nigeria. Explain They have links to other terrorist organisations such as al-Qaeda and ISIS and have carried out waves of bombings, assassinations and abductions. [1 KU mark] *Example In 2014 Boko Haram kidnapped 276 girls from their school. This sparked a huge search and international condemnation. A social media campaign called #Bringbackourgirls was launched.* [1 KU mark] *Think and Link Boko Haram have therefore devastated communities and families in Nigeria with their actions and clearly have the upper hand against the Nigerian government who have declared a state of emergency in the areas where Boko Haram are strongest.* [1 evaluation mark]

This paragraph would score **3 marks** because it has used relevant exemplification and higher-order thinking skills. An example of Boko Haram's tactics has been shown and evaluative language has been used to show the impact on communities. However, the evaluation could be expanded further:

> **Higher-order thinking skills: Evaluate**
>
> The international community has helped to find the kidnapped schoolgirls but the UN has warned the Nigerian population are vulnerable to extremism.

This paragraph is better:

Point In a bid to create a separate Islamic state Boko Haram have caused havoc in Nigeria. Explain They have links to other terrorist organisations such as al-Qaeda and ISIS and have carried out waves of bombings, assassinations and abductions. [1 KU mark] *Example In 2014 Boko Haram kidnapped 276 girls from their school. This sparked a huge search and international condemnation. A social media campaign called #Bringbackourgirls was launched.* [1 KU mark] *Think and Link Boko Haram are therefore devastating communities and families in Nigeria with their actions and clearly have the upper hand against the Nigerian government who have declared a state of emergency in the areas where Boko Haram are strongest.* [1 evaluation mark] *Britain and France are among the countries who have sent teams of experts to help find the kidnapped girls,* [1 KU mark] *but the Nigerian government has not been keen to seek outside assistance. This has therefore limited the support other countries can offer.* [1 evaluation mark] *The UN has warned that Boko Haram's grip on Nigeria could worsen as a result of poverty, lack of education and employment opportunities in the country which make the population vulnerable to extremist ideology.* [1 evaluation mark]

This paragraph would score **6 marks** because it has used relevant exemplification and higher-order thinking skills. It has evaluated the impact of Boko Haram on Nigerian communities but extended this further to show the fears for the future. This is then put into the context of the question and a final judgement is made. This paragraph has successfully:

- ✓ included information relevant to the issue and explained this well
- ✓ included relevant and up-to-date examples and evidence – no more than 7 years old
- ✓ evaluated the information and example by making a judgement in reference to the question
- ✓ followed instruction from the question by remembering appropriate information and making a clear decision

Once the other points have been considered using the Point, Explain, Example, Think and Link structure, a short, concise conclusion will also allow you to be awarded evaluation marks. However, remember not to repeat points you have previously made in your answer.

A short evaluative conclusion for this question could be:

Evidently, the issue of terrorism is having a significant impact on several different countries. Europe has witnessed attacks from ISIS, and terror cells have been discovered in France, Belgium and England. ISIS are wreaking havoc in the Middle East causing many people to flee to Europe. This has exacerbated a migrant crisis in Europe, the largest seen since World War Two. The UN and the international community are working together to combat these terror groups, several of whom have pledged allegiance to one another. The threat of terrorism is very real in Europe, the Middle East and Africa.

This paragraph would score 2 evaluative marks. It has summed up the parts of the world most at risk of terrorist attacks and made a judgement about the impact on these areas.

Planning a 20-mark extended response

The 20-mark extended response question can be asked in any section of the exam. There will be only one 20-mark response and you will have a choice of questions. The 20-mark response demands more from you than the 12-mark Analyse and Evaluate questions. In order to achieve full credit, your answer must be first of all longer than your 12-mark responses, contain more relevant knowledge and exemplification, analyse **and** evaluate throughout, and provide an evaluative conclusion

Look at the following examples of 20-mark questions. This list provides a handful of example questions you could be asked in the exam. Bear in mind that there are only so many questions you could be asked but there are many different ways to word the question. Therefore, it is very important to understand what the question is asking you in order to identify relevant examples to analyse and evaluate.

Remember the Golden Rules. The first thing you need to do is identify the **skill** and **issue** you need to address. This will help you determine what you are being instructed to do. Then you must remember a minimum of four and maximum of six points (paragraphs) to apply to your written response. Think of what you learned in that particular area of study that would be relevant to the question. Remember you must balance your answer. You need to include aspects from different points of view. Look at the examples below to help you understand what the questions are asking you to do and how to plan your written response.

Democracy in Scotland and the United Kingdom

Q | Electoral systems do not always provide fair representation and choice for voters.

Discuss the ways in which an electoral system you have studied does not always provide **fair representation** and **choice** for voters.

You should refer to an electoral system used in Scotland **or** the United Kingdom **or** both in your answer. **20 marks**

The issue is fair representation and choice.

This question is instructing you to consider how accurate electoral systems represent voters and give voters a choice.

Points you could include in your answer (minimum 4, maximum 6):

- First Past the Post advantages for fair representation and/or choice
- First Past the Post disadvantages for fair representation and/or choice
- Additional Member System advantages for fair representation and/or choice
- Additional Member System disadvantages for fair representation and/or choice
- Single Transferable Vote advantages for fair representation and/or choice
- Single Transferable Vote disadvantages for fair representation and/or choice

Balance: These points will balance your argument because they include advantages and disadvantages.

Q | Individuals and groups in society can influence government decision making.

To what extent are **individuals and groups** in society able to **influence** government decision making?

You should refer to individuals and groups in Scotland **or** the United Kingdom **or** both in your answer. **20 marks**

The issue is the influence of individuals and groups.

This question is instructing you to consider how much pressure groups and individuals can convince governments.

Points you could include in your answer (minimum 4, maximum 6):

- interest groups
- single cause groups
- sectional groups
- insider groups
- outside groups
- methods used by different pressure groups
- successful pressure-group campaigns
- unsuccessful pressure-group campaigns

Balance: These points will balance your argument because they include examples of different kinds of pressure groups as well as evidence of successful and unsuccessful action.

Social Issues in the United Kingdom: Social Inequality in the United Kingdom

Q Answers may refer to Scotland **or** the United Kingdom **or** both.

To what extent is **poverty** a problem in the UK?   **20 marks**

The issue is poverty.

This question is instructing you to consider how much poverty social groups experience. Points you could include in your answer (minimum 4, maximum 6):

- poverty amongst the working-age population
- child poverty
- pensioner poverty
- women in poverty
- ethnic minorities in poverty

Balance: These points will balance your argument because they include examples of different groups who experience poverty.

Q Answers may refer to Scotland **or** the United Kingdom **or** both.

Poverty is the most important factor that **affects health**. **Discuss**.   **20 marks**

The issue is poverty and health.

This question is instructing you to consider how accurate it is to claim that poverty causes ill-health.

Points you could include in your answer (minimum 4, maximum 6):

- the effects of poverty on health
- the effects of lifestyle choices on health
- the effects of biology on health
- the effects of social factors on health

Balance: These points will balance your argument because the answer does not focus solely on the effects of poverty on health, but considers other issues which affect a person's health.

Social Issues in the United Kingdom: Crime and the Law in the United Kingdom

Q   Answers may refer to Scotland **or** the United Kingdom **or** both.

To what extent do people commit crimes as a result of an **addictive personality**?

20 marks

The issue is addictive personality as a cause of crime.

This question is instructing you to consider how much addiction can cause someone to commit crime.

Points you could include in your answer (minimum 4, maximum 6):

- biological theories as a cause of crime including:
- addictive personalities
- mental health
- hormones
- human nature
- sociological theories as a cause of crime including:
- the Strain Theory
- the Labelling Theory
- psychological theories as a cause of crime – the Learning Theory
- other causes of crime including:
- poverty
- peer pressure

Balance: These points will balance your argument because the answer does not focus solely on addictive personality as a cause of crime, but considers other theories on the causes of crime.

Q Answers may refer to Scotland **or** the United Kingdom **or** both.

Non-custodial sentences are more likely to **reduce reoffending** than custodial sentences. **Discuss**.   **20 marks**

The issue is reoffending.

This question is instructing you to consider how accurate it is to claim that non-custodial sentences reduce reoffending whereas prison sentences do not.

Points you could include in your answer (minimum 4, maximum 6):

- success of non-custodial sentencing in reducing reoffending including:
  – ASBOs
  – tags
  – co mmunity service
  – drug treatment and testing orders
  – probation and early release
- success of custodial sentencing in reducing reoffending including:
  – education programmes in prison
  – restorative justice programmes in prison
  – rehabilitation programmes in prison

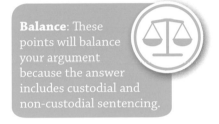

Balance: These points will balance your argument because the answer includes custodial and non-custodial sentencing.

International Issues: Part A: World Powers

Q The political system provides an **effective check** on the government.

Discuss with reference to a world power you have studied.   **20 marks**

The issue is government checks.

This question is instructing you to consider how accurate it is to claim that the government set-up means democracy remains and no one person or group has too much power.

Points you could include in your answer (minimum 4, maximum 6):

World Power – USA

- powers of the President
- ways in which Congress limits the power of the President
- powers of the Supreme Court
- ways in which states can limit the power of the Federal government

Balance: These points will balance your argument because the answer provides information on all the branches of government and does not focus on one area of government.

World Power – China

- lack of effective opposition
- treatment and human rights abuses of political opposition
- control of the media
- grassroots democracy
- Hong Kong's political system

Balance: These points will balance your argument because you are showing the extent to which the CPC controls China, but also there are elements of democracy and opposition within China.

Q **To what extent** in a world power you have studied have some groups achieve **socio-economic success**?   **20 marks**

The issue is socio-economic success.

This question is instructing you to consider how much success social groups achieve in the international country you have studied.

Points you could include in your answer (minimum 4, maximum 6):

Any World Power

The extent to which ethnic minority groups experience inequality and progress in:

- housing
- education
- income and wealth
- crime and justice
- health
- employment

Balance: These points will balance your argument because you are showing the success groups have had in each area but also the inequality they still experience.

International Issues: Part B: World Issues

Q World issues are caused by **social**, **economic** and **political problems**.

Discuss with reference to a world issue you have studied.   **20 marks**

The issue is social, economic and political problems.

This question is instructing you to consider how accurate it is to claim that problems affecting the international community are caused by social, political and economic issues.

World Issue: Development in Africa

Points you could include in your answer (minimum 4, maximum 6):

- social problems including:
  - lack of education
  - -lack of healthcare
- economic problems including
  - debt
  - trade
- political problems including
  - conflict
  - kleptocracy
  - corruption

Balance: These points will balance your argument because you are showing social, economic AND political problems.

Q **To what extent** has a world issue you have studied been resolved by **international organisations**?   **20 marks**

The issue is international organisations.

This question is instructing you to consider how much international organisations help problems affecting the international community.

Points you could include in your answer (minimum 4, maximum 6). Depending on the world issue you studied refer to international organisations such as:

- the United Nations and its associated agencies including:
  - World Health Programme
  - Food and Agriculture Organisation
  - United Nations Children's Fund etc
- the European Union
- the African Union
- the North Atlantic Treaty Organisation
- charities who work to aid those affected by the world issue such as Oxfam and the Red Cross

Balance: These points will balance your argument because you will show the work of more than one international organisation.

Creating a 20-mark extended response

It is important to consider how you will structure your extended response since up to two marks are awarded for structure. An introduction and conclusion are therefore necessary to gain structure marks. You can also be credited for evaluative comments in your conclusion. A short, concise introduction helps you to plan out your answer. You can refer back to your introduction to ensure you remain on track and write what you set out to write about. Example introductions are shown below and example conclusions on pages 69–71. Your essay should be structured in the following way:

> ✓ A concise introduction which sets the scene and outlines what issues will be examined throughout the rest of the answer.
> ✓ Four-to-six paragraphs which follow the Point, Explain, Example, Think and Link structure.
> ✓ A topic sentence at the beginning of each paragraph to make it clear to the reader what issue will be examined in the paragraph.
> ✓ If one issue is mentioned in the question, that should be examined in the first paragraph.
> ✓ A clear conclusion which makes an overall judgement in reference to the question.

An example introduction

Q Electoral systems do not always provide fair representation and choice for voters.

Discuss the ways in which an electoral system you have studied does not always provide **fair representation** and **choice** for voters.

You should refer to an electoral system used in Scotland **or** the United Kingdom **or** both in your answer.

20 marks

There are three distinct electoral systems in operation in the UK. First Past the Post (FPTP) is used to elect members to the House of Commons (MPs); the Additional Member System (AMS) is used to elect members to the Scottish Parliament (MSPs), and Single Transferable Vote (STV) is used to elect local councillors. AMS and STV are proportional systems whereas FPTP is not. Each has its own merits as well as drawbacks in providing fair representation and choice for voters.

This introduction allows the marker to see that you understand where each electoral system is used. By mentioning the systems as well as the issues from the question – fair representation and choice – this introduction shows the intention of the extended response. The answer is going to deal with the advantages/merits and disadvantages/drawbacks of each system in regard to fair representation and choice.

So far we have identified the issues to address and the instructions to follow from example questions, and planned out the points to write about. Once we have set this out in a short introduction, it is time to explain/describe and expand on each point, then analyse and evaluate this information in relation to the question.

SQA principal marking guidelines on 20-mark extended response state:

- Up to **8 marks** will be awarded for demonstration of a candidate's knowledge and understanding (**KU**) – description, explanation and exemplification.
- A **maximum** of **6 marks** available if there is **no accurate or relevant exemplification**.
- A **maximum** of **12 marks** will be awarded for the demonstration of **analysis** and **evaluation** (comments that identify relationships/implications, explore different views or establish consequences/implications) and structured argument (**up to 2 marks for introduction and conclusion**). **4 of the 12 marks are specifically for conclusions**.
- A **maximum** of **6 marks** can be awarded **per point**.
- Where a candidate makes more analytical/evaluative points than are required to gain the maximum allocation of marks, these can be credited as KU marks provided they meet the criteria for this.

The SQA are therefore looking for you to evaluate and analyse your knowledge, so it is important you do not describe the course content and go into storytelling mode. If you do not include relevant exemplification you will lose 14 marks! The best way to approach your response is to consider evidence and examples which are relevant to the points you have decided to include, and consider why this is a good example and what it shows in regard to the issue in the question.

To help you construct your extended response consider the following structure for your points:

PEE then Think and Link!
Point
Explain
Example
Think (Analysis)
Link (Evaluate)

You do not need to follow the above structure strictly when writing your paragraph, but you should most definitely aim to include each element (Point, Explain, Example, Think and Link). The following example answers will make this clear.

Consider evidence or an example (a piece of legislation/report/statistic/person) and explain what this shows in relation to the issue in the question.

Referring to the example extended response questions we planned out earlier, we shall now construct our answers using the Point, Explain, Example, Think and Link structure. Look at the examples below to help you understand the writing structure and how marks are allocated.

Example extended response paragraph 1

Q Electoral systems do not always provide fair representation and choice for voters.

Discuss the ways in which an electoral system you have studied does not always provide **fair representation** and **choice** for voters.

You should refer to an electoral system used in Scotland **or** the United Kingdom **or** both in your answer. **20 marks**

The issue is fair representation and choice.

This question is instructing you to consider how accurate electoral systems represent voters and give voters a choice.

One point we could write about in this answer is:

Additional Member System advantages for fair representation and/or choice.

Let's think of an example or piece of evidence we know that shows the advantages of AMS in regards to fair representation and/or choice.

Higher-order thinking skills: Remember & understand

In the 2016 Scottish Parliament election there were over 20 different political parties to choose from on the various regional lists. People will be represented by different political parties.

Now that you have remembered this piece of information, think about what this shows in regard to representation and/or choice and use this to construct your **'PEE then Think and Link'** paragraph. Make it clear from the first sentence what the paragraph is going to be about:

The Additional Member System (AMS) is the electoral system used in Scottish Parliament elections. Point AMS gives voters more choice. Explain They have two ballot papers – the first one lets voters pick a candidate from a political party to represent their constituency. The second choice voters have is to pick a political party to represent their region. [1 KU mark] Example In the 2016 Scottish Parliament election there were over 20 different political parties to choose from on the various regional lists. [1 KU mark] *Think AMS gave voters a lot of choice in the second ballot.* [1 analysis mark]

This paragraph is weak and would only score **3 marks**. It contains an accurate point with explanation, exemplification and an analytical comment. The analysis is weak and very short. Use your higher-order thinking skills to handle the point in more depth. The information has not been linked to the question either, therefore the information has not been evaluated in reference to the question.

So, we need to think more about our point and exemplification. Remember we have to balance our answer to give opposing views:

Higher-order thinking skills: Analyse & evaluate

AMS wastes few votes. In the 2016 Scottish Parliament election there were over 20 different political parties to choose from on the various regional lists. The Green Party was one party who benefitted from the second vote. **But** voters have no choice in who becomes regional MSP e.g. Kezia Dugdale.

The Additional Member System is used in the Scottish Parliament elections and can be argued to be a system which provides fair representation and choice for voters. Point It provides voters with more choice. Explain Voters are given two ballot papers and can choose individual candidates (79 constituency MSPs are chosen this way) as well as political parties (to choose the regional list MSPs). Since there are two ballot papers, AMS gives voters the opportunity to support a specific party or candidate in one ballot but a different party in another ballot. [1 KU mark] *Example In fact, voters had over 20 different political parties or independent candidates across Scotland for voters to choose from on the various regional lists in 2016. The 2016 election saw many voters choose SNP for the constituency vote and a smaller party such as the Greens in the second vote.* [1 KU mark] *Think AMS allows voters these choices and as a result fewer votes are wasted than if FPTP was used alone, a system in which small parties like the Greens don't succeed.* [1 analysis mark] *However, AMS does not provide voters with the choice of which party members become the regional MSPs. Regional MSPs are less directly accountable to the public than the constituency MSPs, and they have been accused of being second-class MSPs, winning seats more by persuading fellow party members to give them a high position on the party list, rather than because of their appeal to voters.* [1 KU mark] *Example In the 2016 election Scottish Labour leader Kezia Dugdale did not win her constituency seat in Edinburgh Eastern, but she was at the top of the Lothian region list.* [1 KU mark] *Think AMS can therefore be criticised for giving candidates two chances because they can appear on both the constituency and regional list. By placing candidates in constituency and regional votes, political parties can ensure their experienced parliamentarians can still be voted in.* [1 analysis mark] *Link Therefore, AMS gives voters two choices in the ballot but only one choice of an individual candidate, this can be argued as unfair and undemocratic to take the choice away from voters.* [1 evaluation mark]

This paragraph would score the maximum **6 marks** due to the use of relevant exemplification and higher-order thinking skills. The explanation of knowledge has highlighted to the exam marker that you have understood the point that AMS provides voters with more choice. Relevant exemplification has been used to prove this is in fact the case. The extent to which AMS gives the voter a choice is then examined in detail and shows an opposing viewpoint. This is analysis and balance. A further exemplification is provided to show balance and a concluding evaluative comment is made. This paragraph has successfully:

✓ included information relevant to the issue and explained this well
✓ included relevant and up-to-date examples and evidence – no more than 7 years old
✓ analysed the information and example by examining it in detail
✓ balanced the answer by analysing evidence from a different point of view
✓ concluded the point by providing an evaluative comment which shows a judgement has been made
✓ followed instruction from the question by analysing **and** evaluating

Just as shown above, you should aim to build up your extended response techniques and gain more marks as you practise your answers. Start by thinking of a relevant point and a piece of evidence to prove this point, and build your answer from there. It may be a good idea to mark your point, explanation, example, think and link on each of your paragraphs. You could perhaps do this in five different highlighters or colours. Instead, you may wish just to mark P beside your point, EE beside where you have explained and provided example(s), T beside your analysis and evaluation and L beside your link to the question.

By using these techniques, you will be able to check that you have included all the steps and ensure the PEE section of each paragraph is not too long and certainly not longer than your Think and Link section. This is when your response will become too descriptive. Remember 12 of the available 20 marks are allocated to analysis. If your analysis is looking too short, put your higher-order thinking skills hat on and consider what the facts are telling you in regard to the question.

Example extended response paragraph 2

Q Answers may refer to Scotland **or** the United Kingdom **or** both.

To what extent is **poverty** a problem in the UK?   **20 marks**

The issue is poverty.

This question is instructing you to consider how much poverty social groups experience.

One point we could write about in this answer is:

Poverty amongst the working-age population.

Remember to consider the following structure for your points:

PEE then Think and Link!
Point
Explain
Example
Think (Analysis)
Link (Evaluate)

Let's think of an example or piece of evidence we know that shows poverty amongst the working-age population, and we can start to build our answer from here.

Higher-order thinking skills: Remember & understand

The National Living Wage for 25+ year olds in 2016 is £7.20 per hour. The Living Wage Foundation suggests it should be £8.25 per hour.

Point Many working-age adults are known to be income-poor. Explain This means the wage they earn is not high enough to afford a basic but decent standard of living. [1 KU mark] *Example The national living wage for over 25s is £7.20 an hour, £1.05 below the £8.25 suggested by the Living Wage Foundation.* [1 KU mark] *Link Therefore, many who are in full-time work are still in poverty.* [1 evaluation mark]

This paragraph is lacking in information and would only score **3 marks**. It contains an accurate point with explanation and exemplification, but there is no analysis of the facts. The paragraph does however provide an evaluative judgement at the end which links to the question. Unfortunately, the lack of analysis means this information does not actually answer the question as well as it could.

Let's build on our paragraph from here. We need to think more about our point and exemplification. Remember we have to balance our answer to give opposing views:

The Joseph Rowntree Foundation (JRF) states the Minimum Income Standard for a single person is £17,100. The National Minimum Wage and the Living Wage suggested are in fact lower than the minimum standard. **But** the average wage is £26,500 and Britain is rich – Chelsea.

Point Many working-age adults are known to be income-poor. Explain This means the wage they earn is not high enough to afford a basic but decent standard of living. As a result, people can still be in poverty even if they have a full-time job. [1 KU mark] *Example The national living wage is £7.20 an hour, more than £1 below the £8.25 suggested by the Living Wage Foundation. However, the Joseph Rowntree Foundation (JRF) states the Minimum Income Standard for a single person is £17,100 per year.* [1 KU mark] *Think The National Minimum Wage and the Living Wage suggested are in fact much lower than the JRF minimum standard. Therefore, it can be argued that a Living Wage of £8.25 per hour is still not enough to ensure a worker does not fall below the poverty line.* [1 analysis mark] *But many working-age adults do not fall below the poverty line. Example In fact, the average UK wage is £26,500.* [1 KU mark] *Think This is considerably above the JRF minimum standard. Britain is one of the world's richest countries and places such as Kensington and Chelsea (as documented on the reality TV programme Made in Chelsea) are home to very wealthy people.* [1 evaluation mark] *Link Therefore, it can be said that those who earn less than £8 per hour may live in poverty, but the majority of working-age adults earn more than this.* [1 evaluation mark]

This paragraph would score the maximum **6 marks** due to the use of relevant exemplification and higher-order thinking skills. The explanation of knowledge has highlighted to the exam marker your understanding of poverty wages. Relevant exemplification has been used to show this. The reasons for working-age poverty have been examined in detail and an opposing viewpoint has been highlighted to show this is not the case for all. This is analysis and balance. A further exemplification is provided to show the balance, and a concluding evaluative comment is made. This paragraph has successfully:

- ✓ included information relevant to the issue and explained this well
- ✓ included relevant and up-to-date examples and evidence – no more than 7 years old
- ✓ analysed the information and example by examining it in detail
- ✓ balanced the answer by analysing evidence from a different point of view
- ✓ concluded the point by providing an evaluative comment which shows a judgement has been made
- ✓ followed instruction from the question by analysing **and** evaluating

From this example extended response paragraph you can see that in order to build up an answer you can provide more exemplification but only if you **Think** about it. If you simply list lots of relevant and up-to-date facts you will not score any analytical marks. Provide examples but illustrate what the exemplification shows in regard to the question.

Example extended response paragraph 3

Q Answers may refer to Scotland **or** the United Kingdom **or** both.

To what extent do people commit crimes as a result of an **addictive personality**?

20 marks

The issue is addictive personality as a cause of crime.

This question is instructing you to consider how much addiction can cause someone to commit crime.

One point we were going to consider in this answer was:

Biological theories as a cause of crime – addictive personalities.

Remember to consider the following structure for your points:

PEE then Think and Link!
Point
Explain
Example
Think (Analysis)
Link (Evaluate)

Let's think of an example or piece of evidence we know that shows addiction can cause crime, and we can start to build our answer from here.

Higher-order thinking skills: Remember & understand

Addictive personalities can be genetic. Research by the Institute of Alcohol Studies shows that alcohol accounts for over 40% of all violent crime in 2013.

Point There are many causes of crime, depending on the circumstances. Biological factors such as an 'addiction gene' can influence someone's behaviour. Explain Due to their genetic make-up some people are more prone to develop an addiction to perhaps alcohol or drugs. [1 KU mark] Example This can impact crime, as research by the Institute of Alcohol Studies shows that alcohol accounts for over 40% of all violent crime in 2013. [1 KU mark] Think Alcohol can change the way

a person behaves and they could get involved in a fight and assault someone. [1 analysis mark]
Link Evidence shows people are more likely to commit crimes when drunk. [1 evaluation mark]

This paragraph is good and would score **4 marks**. The information has been explained and a relevant and valid example has been used. The use of higher-order thinking skills has put alcohol and crime into context and clarified a type of crime which can result from alcohol consumption. This has then been linked to the question.

But this paragraph could be even better if we think more about the examples we have already remembered and provide more balance:

> **Higher-order thinking skills: Analyse & evaluate**
>
> Addictive personalities can be genetic. Research by the Institute of Alcohol Studies shows that alcohol accounted for over 40% of all violent crime in 2013. There have been over a million alcohol-related crimes each year for the past decade. **But** are addictions nature or nurture?

This paragraph is better:

Point It has been widely accepted by academics, criminologists and even politicians that alcohol influences deviant behaviour. Explain Studies have shown a person can be genetically more prone to developing an addiction to substances such as alcohol or drugs, both of which may influence a person's behaviour, and/or anger management issues resulting in criminal behaviour. [1 KU mark] *Example Research by the Institute of Alcohol Studies shows that alcohol accounted for over 40% of all violent crime in 2013. Furthermore, there have been over a million alcohol-related crimes each year for the past decade.* [2 KU marks] *Think Therefore, a person's susceptibility to alcohol consumption can greatly influence their ability to commit a violent crime. Also, it is well documented that those with a drug-use dependency are more likely to be arrested for theft, burglary and other crimes that will help support their addiction. Therefore, the question remains: do people commit crime because they are genetically prone to addictions (nature) or because they have made bad choices in their life and become addicted to substances (nurture)?* [2 analytical marks] *Link Whether it is nature or nurture, it is clear addiction and addictive personalities can influence a person's susceptibility to commit crime.* [1 evaluation mark]

This paragraph would score the maximum **6 marks** due to the use of relevant exemplification and higher-order thinking skills. The explanation of knowledge has highlighted to the exam marker you are aware of the impact alcohol and drugs have on crime rates and the types of crimes committed associated with addiction. Relevant exemplification has been used to show this. The examples have been examined in detail. The reference to the nature/nurture debate shows a degree of balance and provides successful linkage to the following paragraphs which will deal with other causes. This will provide balance to the overall answer. This paragraph has successfully:

✓ included information relevant to the issue and explained this well
✓ included relevant and up-to-date examples and evidence – no more than 7 years old
✓ analysed the information and example by examining it in detail
✓ balanced the answer by analysing evidence from a different point of view
✓ concluded the point by providing an evaluative comment which shows a judgement has been made
✓ followed instruction from the question by analysing **and** evaluating

Example extended response paragraph 4

Q The political system provides an **effective check** on the government.

Discuss with reference to a world power you have studied.   **20 marks**

The issue is government checks.

This question is instructing you to consider how accurate it is to claim that the government set-up means democracy remains and no one person or group has too much power.

World Power: The United States of America

One point we were going to consider in this answer was:

Ways Congress limits the power of the President.

Remember to consider the following structure for your points:

PEE then Think and Link!
Point
Explain
Example
Think (Analysis)
Link (Evaluate)

Let's think of an example or piece of evidence we know that shows Congress can limit the power of the President and we can start to build our answer from here.

Higher-order thinking skills: Remember & understand

Congress writes, amends and rejects laws. The Senate has rejected further gun control.

Point The Constitution gives Congress the power to write, amend and reject laws. Explain Proposed laws are debated in the House of Representatives as well as the Senate. [1 KU mark] *Example The Senate voted against tighter gun laws. This was something President Obama wanted to change.* [1 KU mark]

This paragraph is lacking depth. Although it has a valid example it has not analysed the example in relation to the question. Higher-order thinking skills have not been used.

This paragraph is better:

The President is the Chief Legislator and introduces new laws. Point The Constitution is clear in giving Congress the power to write laws and the President a duty to faithfully execute these laws. Explain Congress therefore has the power to reject or amend laws suggested by the President. They debate laws in the House of Representatives and in the Senate. [1 KU mark] *Example The Senate rejected President Obama's proposals to introduce tougher gun restrictions following the Sandy Hook Elementary School massacre in 2012.* [1 KU mark] *Think This shows that the President does not have complete power over new laws and must get Congress to agree with him.* [1 analysis mark] *Link The powers outlined in the Constitution therefore provide a check on government.* [1 evaluation mark]

This paragraph is good and would score **4 marks**. The information has been explained and a relevant and valid example has been used. The use of higher-order thinking skills has shown that in order for a new law to be introduced, Congress and the President must agree. This has then been linked to the question.

But this paragraph could be even better if we think more about the examples we have already remembered and provide balance:

Higher-order thinking skills: Analyse and evaluate

Congress writes, amends and rejects laws and only Congress can pass constitutional amendments. The Senate has rejected further gun control. **But** the President can issue Executive Orders – immigration.

The President is the Chief Legislator and introduces new laws. Point The Constitution is clear in giving Congress the power to write laws and the President a duty to faithfully execute these laws. Explain Congress therefore has the power to reject or amend laws suggested by the President. They debate laws in the House of Representatives and in the Senate. [1 KU mark] *Example The Senate rejected President Obama's proposals to introduce tougher gun restrictions following the Sandy Hook Elementary School massacre in 2012.* [1 KU mark] *Think This shows that the President does not have complete power over new laws and must get Congress to agree with him.* [1 analysis mark] *Link The powers outlined in the Constitution therefore provide a check on government.* [1 evaluation mark] *Point However the President can issue Executive Orders. Explain An Executive Order is an order given to Congress by the President to change an existing law. It does not need to be approved by Congress.* [1 KU mark] *Think This power means the President can change the law without any check from Congress. Many critics argue that Executive Orders give the President too much power. It is not uncommon for Presidents to change hundreds of laws using Executive Orders throughout their Presidency.* [2 analysis marks] *Link The Constitution therefore allows a check and balance of power on new laws, but not when amending existing laws.* [1 evaluation mark]

This paragraph would score the maximum **6 marks** due to the use of relevant exemplification and higher-order thinking skills. The explanation of knowledge has highlighted to the exam marker you are aware of the law-making process in the American federal political system. Relevant exemplification in regard to gun control has been used to show this. The reference to Executive Orders provides balance and shows an awareness of Presidential legislative power and its criticisms. This paragraph has successfully:

✓ included information relevant to the issue and explained this well
✓ included relevant and up-to-date examples and evidence – no more than 7 years old
✓ analysed the information and example by examining it in detail
✓ balanced the answer by analysing evidence from a different point of view
✓ concluded the point by providing an evaluative comment which shows a judgement has been made
✓ followed instruction from the question by analysing **and** evaluating

---

Example extended response paragraph 5

World issues are caused by **social**, **economic** and **political problems**.

Discuss with reference to a world issue you have studied.   **20 marks**

The issue is social, economic and political problems.

This question is instructing you to consider how accurate it is to claim that problems affecting the international community are caused by social, political and economic issues.

World Issues: Development in Africa

One point we were going to consider in this answer was:

Social problems – lack of healthcare.

Remember to consider the following structure for your points:

PEE then Think and Link!
Point
Explain

Example
Think (Analysis)
Link (Evaluate)

Let's think of an example or piece of evidence we know that relates to lack of healthcare and we can start to build our answer from here.

Higher-order thinking skills: Remember & understand

According to UNICEF the three highest AIDS/HIV rates in the world are in African countries. This impacts communities as the disease mostly affects the working-age population, leaving the elderly and young behind.

Point HIV/AIDS and malaria are some of the biggest killers in Africa. *Explain* These diseases have a serious impact on communities as they kill the working population leaving the elderly and the young, many of the infants becoming infected through breastfeeding. [1 KU mark] *Example* The three highest AIDS/HIV rates in the world are in the African countries of Swaziland, Botswana and Lesotho. [1 KU mark] *Think* These countries are poor as a result of an ill population. [1 analysis mark] *Link* Poverty is caused by poor health. [1 evaluation mark]

This paragraph contains relevant facts which are good, but the analysis is lacking. This paragraph would score **4 marks** for explanation, exemplification and an analysis comment.

We need to use this information to build on our paragraph to score more marks. We need to think more about the examples we have already remembered.

Higher-order thinking skills: Analyse & evaluate

According to UNICEF the three highest AIDS/HIV rates in the world are in African countries. This impacts communities as the disease mostly affects the working-age population, leaving the elderly and young behind. Poor health also impacts the economy – GDP and agriculture. The lack of healthcare also hinders the problem.

Point HIV/AIDS and malaria are some of the biggest killers in Africa. *Explain* These diseases have a serious impact on communities and the economy. HIV/AIDS kill the working population which leaves the elderly and the young (many of the infants becoming infected through breastfeeding). [1 KU mark] *Example* The three highest AIDS/HIV rates in the world are in the African countries of Swaziland, Botswana and Lesotho. This seriously affects the life expectancy which is very low in each country. [1 KU mark] *Think* A sick population puts pressure on a country and hinders *development as a healthy workforce is vital. The lack of workers through ill-health results in low production and GDP. [2 analysis marks] Example It is estimated that by 2020, Mozambique's agricultural workforce will be 20% smaller than it would have been without HIV/AIDS. [1 KU mark] Think This in turn will have a damaging effect on food supplies and business. [1 analysis mark] Link Poverty in African countries is created by a host of problems. Social problems like health impact the communities of developing countries but also damage the economy by preventing the country from working their way out of poverty. [2 evaluation marks]*

This paragraph would score the maximum **6 marks** due to the use of relevant exemplification and higher-order thinking skills. The explanation of knowledge has highlighted to the exam marker you are aware that ill-health has social as well as economic implications. Relevant exemplification has been used to show this. The reference to healthcare also shows an awareness of the extent and complexity of the problem of ill-health in causing poverty. The following paragraphs will provide balance by discussing other social, economic and political causes of poverty in Africa. This paragraph has successfully:

✓   included information relevant to the issue and explained this well
✓   included relevant and up-to-date examples and evidence – no more than 7 years old
✓   analysed the information and example by examining it in detail
✓   concluded the point by providing an evaluative comment which shows a judgement has been made
✓   followed instruction from the question by analysing **and** evaluating

Examples of 20-mark extended response conclusions

Throughout your extended response, you will be providing an evaluative comment when you link your point, explanation, example and analysis (thinking) to the question as shown in the examples above. However, you should provide an overall evaluative judgement at the end. In other words, sum up your points and answer the question. As you have seen, there is more than one answer in your response. In fact, there are between four and six answers – one in each paragraph you have included. Therefore, your evaluative conclusion will always be along the same theme:

More than one issue/factor contributes or affects the topic in question.

Look at the example conclusions below for questions we have already attempted to answer.

Example conclusion 1

Q | Electoral systems do not always provide fair representation and choice for voters.

Discuss the ways in which an electoral system you have studied does not always provide **fair representation** and **choice** for voters.

You should refer to an electoral system used in Scotland **or** the United Kingdom **or** both in your answer.   **20 marks**

The issue is fair representation and choice.

This question is instructing you to consider how accurate electoral systems represent voters and give voters a choice. Consider the following points:

- FPTP advantages for fair representation and choice
- FPTP disadvantages for fair representation and choice
- AMS advantages for fair representation and choice
- AMS disadvantages for fair representation and choice
- STV advantages for fair representation and choice
- STV disadvantages for fair representation and choice

In conclusion, FPTP does not give voters choice because they can only vote for one candidate. AMS is more proportional and gives voters two choices. It is designed to lead to more of a rainbow parliament, so people will be represented better. STV is even more proportional and voters can choose as many candidates as they like.

This conclusion would score **2 marks**. It refers to choice and provides an overall judgement statement on each voting system, but it neglects the issue of representation from the question. Also the conclusion makes no overall judgement as to which electoral system offers more representation and/or choice.

This conclusion is better:

To conclude, FPTP is not proportional and therefore does not offer the voter a wide choice because they can only pick one candidate in their constituency. The winning party can gain power from a minority of votes which is unrepresentative of the nation. AMS on the other hand is more proportional whilst still giving the voter a directly elected MSP. But the voter has no say in the party lists which are controlled by the political parties. This can be argued to be undemocratic. STV is the most proportional and provides voters with a wide choice. On the other hand it creates coalitions, which leads to compromising politics which is not always representative. Of all the UK voting systems in operation, FPTP is the least representative overall and provides only one choice for voters.

This conclusion would score **4 marks**. It is balanced because it mentions strengths and weaknesses of all the electoral systems. It sums up each system referring to the issues of representation and choice which were featured in the question. It makes a final judgement at the end. This conclusion has therefore evaluated the evidence and answered the question.

Example conclusion 2

Q Answers may refer to Scotland **or** the United Kingdom **or** both.

To what extent is **poverty** a problem in the UK?   **20 marks**

The issue is poverty.

Consider the following points:

- working-age poverty
- child poverty
- pensioner poverty
- women in poverty
- ethnic minority poverty

To conclude, poverty is a problem in the UK for people on low wages and women and ethnic minorities who face discrimination. Changes to the benefit system in recent years have put more children and pensioners in poverty.

This conclusion would score **1 mark**. It mentions all the social groups which were analysed in the response, but provides no overall judgement. The conclusion is not balanced and suggests that only the social groups mentioned experience poverty.

This conclusion is better:

It is clear therefore that poverty is a problem for some vulnerable groups in the UK. The austerity measures and changes to the benefit system have reduced the incomes of many families and pensioners across the UK. Food banks are now a feature of many communities. The UK national minimum wage (NMW) has been criticised for not being a 'living wage' and therefore work does not pay. However the Chancellor announced an increased in minimum wage rates and a living wage for those aged 25 and over. Despite government legislation, discrimination in the workplace against minorities and women is still evident. But despite difficulties faced by many people, the average wage in the UK remains considerably higher than the NMW and the UK is one of the world's richest countries. There is more wealth in the UK than poverty.

This conclusion would score **4 marks**. It sums up the difficulties faced by each group but balances this out by stating the wealth in the UK. The conclusion ends with a final judgement.

Summary: what to remember for knowledge-based questions

12-Mark Questions

Analyse questions are worth a total of **12 marks**:	**Evaluate** questions are worth a total of **12 marks**:
8 = knowledge marks	8 = knowledge marks
4 = analysis marks	4 = evaluate marks
✓ Topic Sentences	✓ Topic Sentences
✓ 3-4 paragraphs – Point Explain Example Think (Analysis)	✓ 3-4 paragraphs – Point Explain Example Think and Link (Evaluate)
✗ No conclusion or mini-conclusions	✓ Conclusion or mini-conclusions

20-Mark Questions

20-mark extended response

To what extent.../Discuss

8 = knowledge

6 = analysis

4 = evaluate

2 = structure

✓ Introduction, conclusion, paragraphs

✓ 4-6 points with mini-conclusions – Point, Explain, Example, Think and Link

✓ Full intro – Background (context), factors, line of argument

✓ Full conclusion – give an overall judgement, go through the factors with brief analysis

CHAPTER 2

The Higher Modern Studies exam paper: source-based questions

Source-based questions may appear in any section of the paper and the content of the sources could be something you have never studied before. Do not worry if this is the case. Your own knowledge may be useful for analysis of information but it is not required in your answer. You will not be credited for adding your own knowledge to your answer. Your answers must be based solely on the information from the sources; therefore, the answers are right there in front of you!

Types of skills-based questions

There are two types of source-based questions: conclusion and objectivity. Each is worth 8 marks, so will account for 16 of the possible 60 marks available in the exam paper. Both questions test two types of skills: higher-order thinking and research skills.

The higher order thinking skill is **evaluating**. You have to make a judgement using the sources.

Higher-order thinking skills: Evaluation

I must make a judgement about what the information in the sources is telling me.

The research skill is **synthesising**. This means you need to combine information from various sources. In other words, find information in one source which supports or contradicts information from another part of the same source or a different source. You are aiming to link up information from one place to another. The questions will have at least two sources and these will be a mix of written and statistical sources.

A conclusion question will ask you to draw conclusions on specific issues from the sources then make a further overall conclusion. A conclusion is a judgement and summary of what the sources are telling you. The specific issues will be listed as bullet points in the question. For example:

Q What conclusions can be drawn from the results of the elections? You must draw conclusions about:
  • the success of the Labour Party
  • the success of other parties.
You must give an overall conclusion on the results of the election in the UK.   **8 marks**

The objectivity question will ask you to consider the accuracy of a statement based on the information from the sources. In other words, you have to detect the degree to which the statement is objective. This means the extent to which the statement is based on facts from the sources. This will be in the form of a statement. For example:

> **Q** To what extent is it accurate to state that President Obama's foreign policy is popular with the US public? **8 marks**

> **⚠** **WARNING!** Remember this is a source-based question and different to the 'To what extent...' 20-mark extended response. You must base your answer solely on the sources given; do not add in any of your own knowledge. However you can use your own knowledge to help you analyse the information in the sources.

> ✓ The objectivity question is worth 8 marks. Up to 2 marks are available for evaluating the reliability of sources.

Evaluating data in source-based questions

As part of the source-based questions you will be expected to evaluate data sources and the reliability of the given sources. Learning how to evaluate data sources and their reliability, and identify relevant information will also help you in your research for your assignment. There are various ways in which data can be displayed. It is important you know how to read data charts and graphs and evaluate the information to help you in your task.

When evaluating data it is important to do the following:

- ✓ Identify a trend – is there an increase/decrease in the numbers or have they remained constant?
- ✓ Group relevant information together.
- ✓ Make comparisons – compare numbers from different parts of the diagram and conclude what this shows.
- ✓ Spot any anomalies – missing data or low sample size.
- ✓ Recalculate data to help summarise what the figures show.
- ✓ Conclude overall what the data shows.

> ## Word bank
>
> **Data sample:** this refers to the number of people surveyed. If the number is low then the conclusions drawn from the data are not as reliable. The higher the sample size the better. For example a sample size of 1000 is a decent number.

Some useful words and phrases to describe trends and make comparisons are shown below. You can see how these have been used in the example evaluations which follow:

- decreased, dropped, declined, fell, went down, fell sharply, less
- increased, rose, went up, rose sharply, more
- remained constant, remained steady, remained stable, remained unchanged
- steadily increased/decreased, gently increased/decreased
- peaked, reached its highest level, sank to its lowest level
- highest, lowest, compared with, equally, similarly, likewise
- alternatively, yet, but, although, on the other hand, whereas
- majority, minority, wide gap, most common, least common

You can also describe the figures as fractions instead of percentages. Look at the examples of data display and evaluation below.

Data tables

A data table is statistical information displayed using columns and rows. The tables may contain only a few rows or columns or can have several rows and columns. The data may contain percentages, whole numbers or positive and negative numbers

Table 2.1: Change in Political Party share of the vote by percentage point

	99–03 difference		03–07 difference		07–11 difference		11–16 difference	
	Const	Region	Const	Region	Const	Region	Const	Region
SNP	−4.9	−6.4	9.1	10.2	12.5	13.0	1.1	−2.3
Cons	1.1	0.1	0.0	−1.6	−2.7	−1.5	8.1	10.6
Labour	−4.1	−4.3	−2.5	−0.2	−0.5	−2.8	−9.2	−7.2
Green	0.0	3.3	0.1	−2.9	−0.1	0.3	0.6	2.2
LibDems	1.1	−0.6	0.8	−0.5	−8.2	−6.1	−0.1	0.0

Source: SPICe Briefing Election 2016, Scottish Parliament, 11th May 2016

The title clearly states the data table is showing figures in reference to the share of votes for each political party over time.

The headings of the columns clearly show the election years that are compared in that column. Both constituency and regional results are included.

The data is shown in percentage points. A negative number indicates a decrease and a positive number indicates an increase.

The Liberal Democrats regional vote decreased by 6.1% in 2011, compared to the election result of 2007.

The SNP's constituency vote increased by 1.1% in 2016 from 2011.

Evaluating the data table

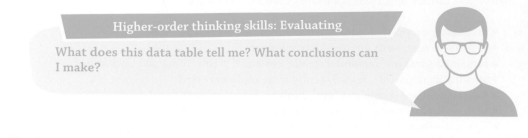

Higher-order thinking skills: Evaluating

What does this data table tell me? What conclusions can I make?

The Conservatives had the **largest increase** of both constituency and regional votes in 2016 compared to 2011 with 8.1% and 10.6% respectively. Labour was the only party to **decrease** its share of votes in both the constituency and regional results in 2016. However this has been the **consistent trend** for Labour since devolution in 1999, as their share of constituency and regional votes have **declined** in each election. The table shows the SNP have **increased** their share of the constituency vote in each election since 2003 with their **biggest gain** in the 2011 election. In 2016 the Green party got their **largest** share of constituency votes since 1999, and their **biggest** share of regional votes since 2003.

Overall this data table shows:

- Since 2003 the SNP have increased their share of constituency and regional votes in each election with the exception on 2016's regional vote.
- Since 1999 the SNP have increased their share of both constituency and regional votes, particularly in the 2011 election.
- As the SNP have become more popular in Scotland since 1999, Labour continues to lose votes in each election.
- The Conservative party had the largest gains in both constituency and regional votes than any other party in 2016.

Evaluating the reliability of the source

The source has been produced by the **Scottish Parliament**. The research has been carried out by professional researchers and published shortly after the election took place. The table is therefore unbiased and contains factual information. This makes it a reliable source.

Bar graphs

A bar graph is statistical information displayed using bars drawn either horizontally or vertically. The example below shows a vertical bar graph display.

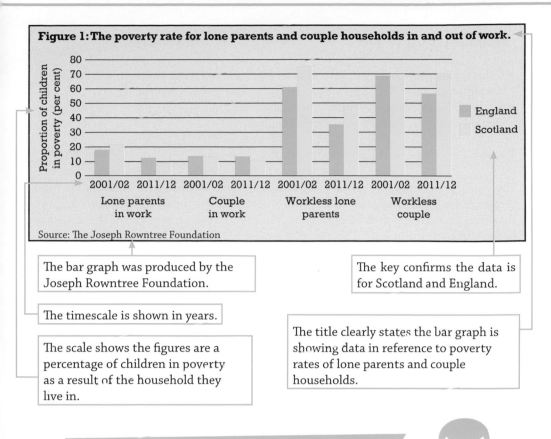

Figure 1: The poverty rate for lone parents and couple households in and out of work.

Source: The Joseph Rowntree Foundation

The bar graph was produced by the Joseph Rowntree Foundation.

The key confirms the data is for Scotland and England.

The timescale is shown in years.

The scale shows the figures are a percentage of children in poverty as a result of the household they live in.

The title clearly states the bar graph is showing data in reference to poverty rates of lone parents and couple households.

Higher-order thinking skills: Evaluating

What does this bar graph tell me? What conclusions can I make?

Evaluating the bar graph data

The percentage of children in poverty in households where lone parents work is **higher** in Scotland (21%) than in England (18%) for 2000/01. But in 2011/12 the figures are **lower for both** Scotland and England, but this time England has a **higher** percentage of children in poverty than Scotland with 12% **compared** to 9%. There are more children in poverty in households where the lone parent is workless. This rate was 75% in Scotland in 2001/02 and 60% in England. **Both figures fell** to 49% in Scotland and 35% in England in 2011/12.

The percentage of children in poverty in households where a couple works is **similar** for both Scotland and England in 2001/02 at around 12 and 13% respectively. This figure **drops slightly** to 10% in Scotland but **remains unchanged** in England for 2011/12. Poverty is **higher** in workless couple households than those in work. In 2001/02 Scotland had **slightly more** poverty in workless couple households than England with 70% **compared** to 68%. This figure **dropped** to 57% in England for 2011/12 but **remained unchanged** in Scotland.

Overall this bar graph shows:

- Poverty rates have not increased between 2001 and 2012 but have either decreased or remained constant for both lone parent and couple households.
- In 2001/02 workless lone-parent households had the highest poverty rates, but in 2011/12 this has changed to workless couples.

Evaluating the reliability of the source

The **Joseph Rowntree Foundation** is a respected independent organisation who campaign for social change and carry out research. They regularly publish their findings including their annual calculations on the Minimum Income Standard which has helped to introduce the living wage. This data is therefore reliable.

Bar graphs can also be shown 'stacked' (see figure below). This means there is one bar with colour-coded or shaded sections to show different figures.

10 Biggest Critics and Fans of the U.S.

Views of the U.S.

Top 10 Critics	Unfavorable	Favorable
Egypt	85%	10%
Jordan	85	12
Turkey	73	19
Russia	71	23
Palest ter.	66	30
Greece	63	34
Pakistan	59	14
Lebanon	57	41
Tunisia	47	42
Germany	47	51
Top 10 Fans		
Philippines	6	92
Israel	16	84
South Korea	17	82
Kenya	12	80
El Salvador	15	80
Italy	18	78
Ghana	9	77
Vietnam	18	76
Bangladesh	22	76
Tanzania	14	75
France	25	75

Source: Spring 2014 Global Attitudes survey. Q15a
PEW RESEARCH CENTER

Stacked bar graphs are good to show different data for groups instead of drawing multiple bar graphs for each set of data.

Line graph

A line graph is statistical information displayed using lines. The example below shows a single line on the graph, but line graphs can display multiple lines which are either colour-coded or labelled.

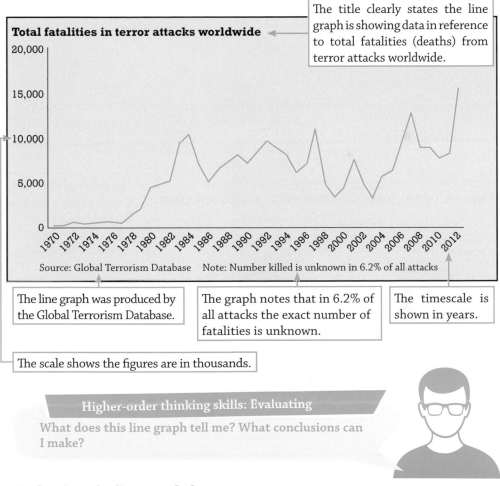

The title clearly states the line graph is showing data in reference to total fatalities (deaths) from terror attacks worldwide.

Total fatalities in terror attacks worldwide

Source: Global Terrorism Database   Note: Number killed is unknown in 6.2% of all attacks

The line graph was produced by the Global Terrorism Database.

The graph notes that in 6.2% of all attacks the exact number of fatalities is unknown.

The timescale is shown in years.

The scale shows the figures are in thousands.

Higher-order thinking skills: Evaluating

What does this line graph tell me? What conclusions can I make?

Evaluating the line graph data

There are **more** fatalities worldwide from terror attacks in 2012 compared to 1970. There were just over 15,000 fatalities in 2012 **compared** to only a few hundred in 1970. The years in which the numbers of fatalities **rose sharply** include 1984, 1997, 2001, 2007 and 2012. In the 5 years **between** 2002 and 2007 the number of terror fatalities **continued to rise** but then **fell** until 2010 when they **very sharply rose** to their **highest** in 2012.

Overall this line graph shows:

- Although the figures rise and fall throughout the time period, there has been a significant increase in fatalities from terror attacks from 1970 to 2012.
- Terrorism is a greater threat worldwide than 40 years ago.

Evaluating the reliability of the source

The **Global Terrorism Database** is the most comprehensive of its kind. It is an official record of all terrorist attacks. Information is gathered and maintained by professional researchers from the University of Maryland. The database is available to the public via the website. The information shown in the database is therefore reliable and trustworthy.

Pie chart

A pie chart is statistical information displayed in a circular format. The example below shows a pie that is colour-coded to distinguish between the different sections but it can also be shaded and patterned.

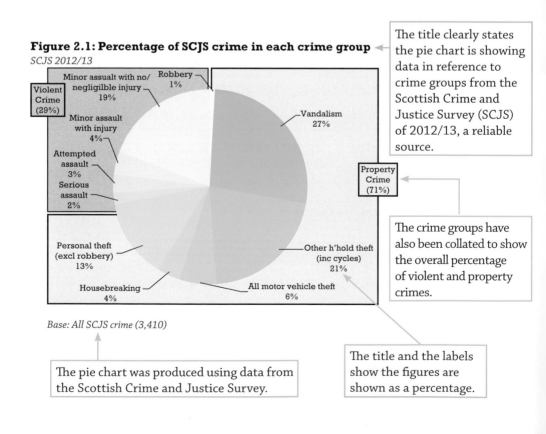

Figure 2.1: Percentage of SCJS crime in each crime group
SCJS 2012/13

The title clearly states the pie chart is showing data in reference to crime groups from the Scottish Crime and Justice Survey (SCJS) of 2012/13, a reliable source.

The crime groups have also been collated to show the overall percentage of violent and property crimes.

Base: All SCJS crime (3,410)

The pie chart was produced using data from the Scottish Crime and Justice Survey.

The title and the labels show the figures are shown as a percentage.

Evaluating the pie chart data

> **Higher-order thinking skills: Evaluating**
>
> What does this pie chart tell me? What conclusions can I make?

The **majority** of crimes are those concerning property (71%) as **opposed to** violent crime (29%). In fact of property crime, vandalism is the **most common** at 27%. There is **more** household theft (21%) **compared** to personal theft (13%). Minor assault makes up nearly **one fifth** of violent crime, with serious assault **accounting for** only 2%.

Overall this pie chart shows:

- Nearly three quarters of all crime concerns property.
- Vandalism is the most common crime.

Evaluating the reliability of the source

The source comes from the **Scottish Crime and Justice Survey** which is commissioned by the Scottish government. The survey is carried out by independent research companies on behalf of the Scottish government. It is a large-scale social survey which conducts face-to-face interviews with randomly selected adults about their experiences and perceptions of crime. The data, like other sources of crime, has its limitations. Crimes which may fit into more than one category are only recorded in one. Furthermore, a person's perception of crime may differ from someone else's. Therefore, the figures from the survey must be treated with caution and are not a true account of crime in Scotland. But the source is useful nonetheless since the sample size is large and it is used to shape and drive policy.

Cartogram

A cartogram is a map which displays statistical information. The example below shows a world map but a cartogram could show a map of anywhere such as Europe, the UK or even a city or town.

The title clearly states the cartogram is showing data in reference to the global image of the USA and China.

The key confirms the data is for the USA and China from various continents worldwide.

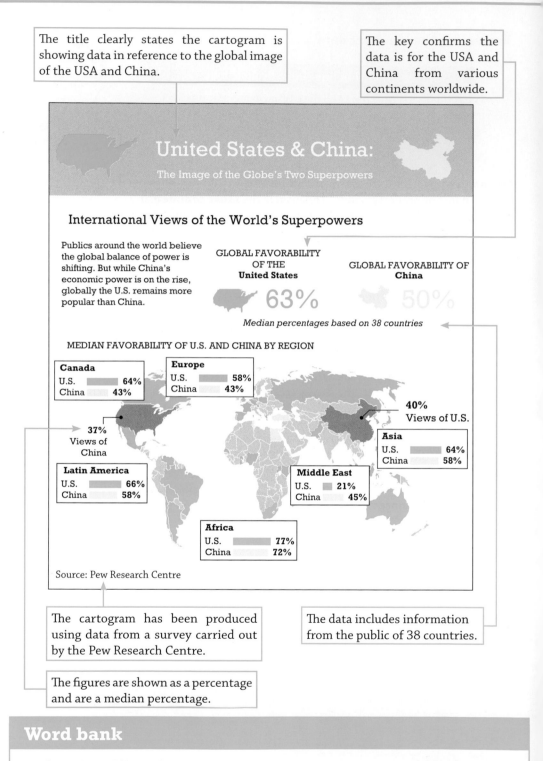

United States & China:
The Image of the Globe's Two Superpowers

International Views of the World's Superpowers

Publics around the world believe the global balance of power is shifting. But while China's economic power is on the rise, globally the U.S. remains more popular than China.

GLOBAL FAVORABILITY OF THE **United States**

63%

GLOBAL FAVORABILITY OF **China**

50%

Median percentages based on 38 countries

MEDIAN FAVORABILITY OF U.S. AND CHINA BY REGION

Canada
U.S. **64%**
China **43%**

Europe
U.S. **58%**
China **43%**

40%
Views of U.S.

37%
Views of China

Asia
U.S. **64%**
China **58%**

Latin America
U.S. **66%**
China **58%**

Middle East
U.S. **21%**
China **45%**

Africa
U.S. **77%**
China **72%**

Source: Pew Research Centre

The cartogram has been produced using data from a survey carried out by the Pew Research Centre.

The data includes information from the public of 38 countries.

The figures are shown as a percentage and are a median percentage.

Word bank

Median: the middle number from the results. One way statisticians use to show the average.

Evaluating the cartogram

> **Higher-order thinking skills: Evaluating**
>
> What does this cartogram tell me? What conclusions can I make?

Overall 63% of people worldwide favour the USA, **whereas** 50% favour China. The USA is viewed **more** favourably than China in the USA, Canada, Europe, Latin America, Africa and Asia. **Whereas** China is viewed **more** favourably in the Middle East and China. In Africa **neither** is favoured particularly **more** than the other with 77% favouring the USA and 72% China. But in the Middle East the **gap is wider** with only 21% favouring the USA and nearly half (45%) favouring China.

Overall this cartogram shows:

- The USA enjoys a more positive world view than China in eight of the surveyed locations.
- In Africa the public view the USA and China almost equally.
- The biggest differences of opinion are in Canada and the Middle East.

Evaluating the reliability of the source

The **Pew Research Centre** is an independent American think-tank which carries out social science research in regard to public opinion, social issues and demographic trends. Their work is highly regarded and therefore deemed reliable.

How to approach a source-based conclusion question:

Step 1: Read the question and identify the issue you have to look for information about. Do not waste vital time in the exam reading the sources first.

Step 2: Read the sources and highlight or underline sentences or partial sentences which are relevant to the issue in the bullet point or the overall conclusion you have to make.

Tip:	It is a good idea to use different colours of highlighters to distinguish between relevant information for each bullet point. Or you could highlight and underline.

Step 3: Review your highlighted sections and look to synthesise the information between the sources i.e. match up and group together information from different parts of the sources. Ensure you have a piece of evidence from every source.

Step 4: Repeat steps 2 and 3 for the second bullet point in the question and the overall conclusion.

Example source-based conclusion question

Here is an example of a source-based conclusion question from Section 3 of the 2015 SQA exam paper which contains three sources:

Question 4

Study Sources A, B and C below and opposite then attempt the question that follows.

SOURCE A

The Recession and The Eurozone

When the Euro launched in 1999 it became the official currency of 11 European Union (EU) member countries. Gradually, more countries saw the Euro's benefits and adopted it as their currency. Today over 336 million people in 19 countries use it and form what we call the Eurozone. Nine EU countries have not joined the Eurozone.

During the recession which began in 2008, the Euro struggled to compete against stronger currencies such as the dollar which led to some countries reporting a series of long-term economic problems.

As a result of the recession, across the EU many businesses lost sales and cut jobs. The unemployment rate throughout the EU went from 7% in 2008 to 10% in 2014 with an estimated 24·5 million people out of work.

Some Eurozone members have required financial hand-outs to help them cope with their growing level of debt. In May 2010 Greece received 110 billion Euros followed by 130 billion Euros in 2012. Ireland and Spain have also benefited from a 90 billion Euro hand-out. Portugal received financial assistance twice within the space of a year. However, some Eurozone countries such as Germany have benefited from using the Euro to build up trade and generate income, which has kept their debt levels comparatively low. In the EU, debt went from 63% of Gross Domestic Product* (GDP) in 2008 to 89% of GDP in 2014.

badly as some other Non-Eurozone members in terms of unemployment. Some other Non-Eurozone countries have not seen big increases in unemployment as many of their young people have moved to other countries in order to find work.

The Eurozone is a huge market for businesses from the United States, China, India, Japan, Russia and other major world economic powers who have been affected by the recession despite not being EU members. In 2008 these five powers purchased 41% of EU exports. By 2014 this figure was 37%. The collapse of the Euro or a situation where countries are unable to repay their debt could trigger a further world-wide recession.

*Gross Domestic Product – total value of goods and services produced in one country

> Source A is a written source. The title suggests it will give us information about the recession. We will find information in this source relevant to all three conclusions.

> Source B is a statistical source in the form of a data table.

SOURCE B

Unemployment Rates (%) — Selected Eurozone Members

Country	(2008)	(2014)
Ireland	6·4	11
Greece	7·7	25.9
Portugal	8·5	15.3
Spain	11·3	25.6
Cyprus	3·7	15.3

Government Debt — Selected Eurozone Members
(National Debt as a Percentage of GDP)

Country	(2008)	(2014)
Ireland	25%	123%
Greece	105%	175%
Portugal	68%	129%
Spain	36%	72%
Cyprus	59%	112%

> Read the headings of statistical sources B and C to quickly determine what information they display.

> Source B shows the unemployment rates and government debt of Eurozone members. This is relevant to the first bullet point and the overall conclusion.

Source C is a statistical source in the form of a data table.

SOURCE C

Unemployment Rates (%) — Selected Non-Eurozone Members

Country	(2008)	(2014)
UK	5.6	6
Sweden	6.2	8.1
Denmark	3.5	7
Poland	7.1	9.2
Romania	5.8	7.2

Government Debt — Selected Non-Eurozone Members
(National Debt as a Percentage of GDP)

Country	(2008)	(2014)
UK	44%	90%
Sweden	40%	40%
Denmark	27%	44%
Poland	45%	57%
Romania	13%	38%

Source C shows the unemployment rates and government debt of non-Eurozone members. This is relevant to the second bullet point and the overall conclusion.

Read the question first. Note the three conclusions you have to make. [Highlight, preferably in different colours or number 1,2,3 the two bullet points in the question and the statement underneath about an overall conclusion.]

Remember, you do not have to have any prior knowledge of the Eurozone or the Euro to answer this question. The sources are written in a way to help you understand the topic.

Attempt the following question, using only the information in Sources A, B and C opposite and above.

What conclusions can be drawn about the impact of the recession on different EU members?

You must draw conclusions about:

• the impact of the recession on Eurozone members

• the impact of the recession on Non-Eurozone members

You must now give an overall conclusion about the impact of the recession on the EU.

Now you have scanned the sources and identified the instruction and issues from the question you must now look to extract relevant information. Remember to **synthesise** – link up information from different sources. The two statistical sources show data for Eurozone members and non-Eurozone members. When reading Source A look for information which relates to the statistical sources.

Question 4

Study Sources A, B and C below and opposite then attempt the question that follows.

SOURCE A

| Relevant to both bullet points. | Relevant to first bullet point. |

The Recession and The Eurozone

When the Euro launched in 1999 it became the official currency of 11 European Union (EU) member countries. Gradually, more countries saw the Euro's benefits and adopted it as their currency. Today over 336 million people in 19 countries use it and form what we call the Eurozone. Nine EU countries have not joined the Eurozone.

During the recession which began in 2008, the Euro struggled to compete against stronger currencies such as the dollar which led to some countries reporting a series of long-term economic problems.

As a result of the recession, across the EU, many businesses lost sales and cut jobs. The unemployment rate throughout the EU went from 7% in 2008 to 10% in 2014 with an estimated 24·5 million people out of work.

Some Eurozone members have required financial hand-outs to help them cope with their growing level of debt. In May 2010 Greece received 110 billion Euros followed by 130 billion Euros in 2012. Ireland and Spain have also benefited from a 90 billion Euro hand-out. Portugal received financial assistance twice within the space of a year. However, some Eurozone countries such as Germany have benefited from using the Euro to build up trade and generate income, which has kept their debt levels comparatively low. In the EU, debt went from 63% of Gross Domestic Product* (GDP) in 2008 to 89% of GDP in 2014.

Largely because of an increase in part-time jobs, the UK's economy has not suffered as badly as some other Non-Eurozone members in terms of unemployment. Some other Non-Eurozone countries have not seen big increases in unemployment as many of their young people have moved to other countries in order to find work.

The Eurozone is a huge market for businesses from the United States, China, India, Japan, Russia and other major world economic powers who have been affected by the recession despite not being EU members. In 2008 these five powers purchased 41% of EU exports. By 2014 this figure was 37%. The collapse of the Euro or a situation where countries are unable to repay their debt could trigger a further world-wide recession.

*Gross Domestic Product – total value of goods and services produced in one country

| Relevant to both bullet points. | Relevant to second bullet point. |

SOURCE B

Unemployment Rates (%) — Selected Eurozone Members

Country	(2008)	(2014)
Ireland	6·4	11
Greece	7·7	25.9
Portugal	8·5	15.3
Spain	11·3	25.6
Cyprus	3·7	15.3

Government Debt — Selected Eurozone Members
(National Debt as a Percentage of GDP)

Country	(2008)	(2014)
Ireland	25%	123%
Greece	105%	175%
Portugal	68%	129%
Spain	36%	72%
Cyprus	59%	112%

Relevant to first bullet point and all have seen the biggest change.

Relevant to overall conclusion.

SOURCE C

Unemployment Rates (%) — Selected Non-Eurozone Members

Country	(2008)	(2014)
UK	5.6	6
Sweden	6.2	8.1
Denmark	3.5	7
Poland	7.1	9.2
Romania	5.8	7.2

Relevant to overall conclusion.

Relevant to second bullet point and all have seen the biggest change.

Government Debt — Selected Non-Eurozone Members
(National Debt as a Percentage of GDP)

Country	(2008)	(2014)
UK	44%	90%
Sweden	40%	40%
Denmark	27%	44%
Poland	45%	57%
Romania	13%	38%

Relevant to overall conclusion.

Attempt the following question, using only the information in Sources A, B and C opposite and above.

What conclusions can be drawn about the impact of the recession on different EU members?

You must draw conclusions about:

• the impact of the recession on Eurozone members

• the impact of the recession on Non-Eurozone members

You must now give an overall conclusion about the impact of the recession on the EU.

Creating an answer

SQA principal marking guidelines on 8 mark source-based conclusion questions:

- For full marks, candidates **must** refer to **all** sources in their answer. A maximum of 6 marks if all sources are not used.
- For full marks, candidates **must make evaluative comments/judgement(s)/ draw a conclusion** about each of the points given in the question.
- **Up to 3 marks** are awarded for appropriate use of evidence depending on the quality of explanation and the synthesis of the evidence to reach any one conclusion.
- **Two** further marks are available for an **overall summative conclusion**.
- For full marks candidates must refer to all sources in their answer.

✓ **Therefore 3 marks are available per conclusion and 2 marks for the overall conclusion = 8 marks.**

Once you have read the sources and identified relevant information you must group this information together to help you form a judgement. You may not need to use all the evidence you have identified in order to gain full marks, there is plenty of information to choose from. You must be careful not to repeat any information in your overall conclusion as you will not be credited twice for the same information.

The impact of the recession on Eurozone members:

Sources A, B and C show that the impact of the recession on Eurozone members has been largely negative.

This answer would score **0 marks** because:

✗ A valid and correct conclusion has been made but no evidence has been shown to explain this conclusion.

A better paragraph about the impact of the recession on Eurozone members:

Source A states that some Eurozone countries such as Greece, Ireland and Portugal required financial hand-outs to help them cope with their increasing debt. Synthesis *Statistical evidence from Source B shows Ireland has seen a 98% increase in their debt, Greece 71% and Portugal 61%.* Conclusion *This shows the recession has had a dramatically negative effect on debt in some Eurozone countries.*

This paragraph would score **2 marks** because:

✓ Relevant evidence has been identified from Source A to show the countries affected.

✓ A data trend has been identified from Source B: debt has increased.

✓ Evidence has been synthesised from Sources A and B. Both sources highlight the rise in debt.

✓ A clear judgement has been made in reference to the bullet point in the question.

This paragraph is better:

Conclusion *The recession has had a negative impact on Eurozone members but not to the same extent for all. Source A shows the unemployment rate across the EU rose to 10% in 2014.* Synthesis *Source B shows five selected EU members all with unemployment rates higher than the EU average, ranging from 11-25.9%. Furthermore, debt across the EU as a whole increased to 89% GDP in 2014 (Source A). Source B shows that while all five selected EU members' debt levels rose, Ireland's increased the most by 98%. Meanwhile, although Spain's debt level increased by 36% it was still below the EU average.*

This paragraph would score **3 marks** because:

✓ Relevant evidence has been identified from Source A and synthesised with Source B.

✓ Figures have been summarised, calculated and compared. A data trend has also been indentified.

✓ An insightful judgement has been made in reference to the bullet point in the question.

The impact of the recession on Non-Eurozone members:

Conclusion The impact of the recession was not as severe on non-Eurozone members. Synthesis In 2014 of the selected non-Eurozone members Poland had the highest unemployment rate of 9.2% (Source C) which is still below the EU average of 10% (Source A).

This paragraph would score **2 marks** because:

✓ Relevant evidence has been identified and sysnthesised from Sources A and C.
✓ A data trend has been identified from Source C to show debt is below the overall average.
✓ A clear judgement has been made in reference to the bullet point in the question.

This paragraph is better:

Conclusion The recession had a lesser impact on non-Eurozone members. Debt is higher for Eurozone members than non-Eurozone. Synthesis Statistical evidence shows selected Eurozone members have debt between 72 and 175% of their GDP compared to non-Eurozone members whose debt ranges between 38 and 90%. In fact Sweden's debt (non-Eurozone) remained the same between 2008 and 2014. Although the UK's debt has increased to 90% they have the lowest unemployment rate (6%) of all the selected Eurozone and non-Eurozone members and also lower than the EU average of 10%. According to Source A this is largely because of an increase in part-time jobs and so the UK's economy has not suffered as badly as some other non-Eurozone members.

This paragraph would score **3 marks** because:

✓ Relevant evidence has been identified from Source A, B and C.
✓ Conclusions have been made about the data from statistical sources B and C as it has been grouped together to show the range of figures.
✓ Evidence has been synthesised from Sources A, B and C.
✓ An insightful judgement has been made in reference to the bullet point in the question.

An overall conclusion

When providing an overall conclusion it is important to avoid repeating the same information you have already stated. If you do this you will not have made a new overall conclusion. Evaluate the answers you have given for each point and make a judgement.

> **Tip:** Look for information you may have highlighted previously but did not use because it did not synthesise with the other sources.

Look at the example below which shows a full answer followed by an overall conclusion:

Conclusion *The recession has had a negative impact on Eurozone members but not to the same extent for all. Source A shows the unemployment rate across the EU rose to 10% in 2014.* Synthesis *Source B shows five selected EU members all with unemployment rates higher than the EU average, ranging from 11-25.9%. Furthermore, debt across the EU as a whole increased to 89% GDP in 2014 (Source A). Source B shows that while all five selected EU members' debt levels rose, Ireland's increased the most by 98%. Meanwhile, although Spain's debt level increased by 36% it was still below the EU average.*

Conclusion *The recession had a lesser impact on non-Eurozone members. Debt is higher for Eurozone members than non-Eurozone.* Synthesis *Statistical evidence shows selected Eurozone members have debt between 72 and 175% of their GDP compared to non-Eurozone members whose debt ranges between 38 and 90%. In fact Sweden's debt (non-Eurozone) remained the same between 2008 and 2014. Although the UK's debt has increased to 90% they have the lowest unemployment rate (6%) of all the selected Eurozone and non-Eurozone members and also lower than the EU average of 10%. According to Source A this is largely because of an increase in part-time jobs and so the UK's economy has not suffered as badly as some other non-Eurozone members.*

Conclusion *Overall the EU was badly affected by the recession but Eurozone members suffered more than non-Eurozone members.* Synthesis *Source A shows EU exports decreased by 4% and across the EU many businesses lost sales and cut jobs. This saw large increases in unemployment and national debt in Eurozone countries such as Greece who required 240 billion Euros in financial assistance to cope with its 25.9% unemployment rate and 175% national debt. No non-Eurozone countries required financial bail-outs.*

The overall conclusion would score the available **2 marks** because:

> ✓ An evaluative judgment has been made about the impact of the recession on the EU as a whole.
> ✓ Evidence has been synthesised within Source A and with Sources B and C.
> ✓ There is no repetition from the previous paragraphs.

How to approach a source-based objectivity question:

Step 1: Read the question and identify the issue you have to look for information about. Do not waste vital time in the exam reading the sources first.

Step 2: Read the sources and highlight or underline sentences or partial sentences which either show the statement to be accurate or inaccurate.

> **Tip:** It is a good idea to use different colours of highlighter to distinguish between relevant information which shows accuracy and inaccuracy. Or you could highlight and underline.

Step 3: Review your highlighted sections and look to synthesise the information between the sources i.e. match up and group together information from different parts of the sources. Ensure you have a piece of evidence from every source.

Step 4: Look for information about the authorship of the sources. Look to see if the information has been provided by well-known research companies, official government departments, newspapers etc. Look for information regarding sample size and geographical location if a survey method was used.

> **Tip:** Learn more about reliable sources in Chapter 3.

Example source-based objectivity question

Here is an example of a source-based objectivity question from Section 1 of the SQA specimen exam paper which contains two sources:

Question 1

Study Sources A and B below and opposite then attempt the question that follows.

SOURCE A

The 2010 General Election televised debates

The 2010 General Election witnessed the first live television debates between leaders from each of the three main UK parties — Conservatives, Labour and the Liberal Democrats. Cameron, Brown and Clegg all hoped to visually connect with voters during a tightly fought campaign nicknamed the 'digital election'.

Before the first-ever debate of its kind, an Ipsos MORI poll revealed 60% of those voters surveyed felt the TV debates would be important to them in helping decide the way they would vote. The performance of the candidates during the debates could also have the potential to alter the way the media would handle coverage of each of the leaders and their parties. Following the debates, a range of polls suggested Nick Clegg had won convincingly, with many voters indicating they would switch to the Liberal Democrats. The success of Nick Clegg led to claims of 'Cleggmania' and a prediction of a historic increase in the number of seats for the Liberal Democrats.

A second survey conducted after the election by an independent polling organisation found the leaders' TV debates changed the voting intentions of more than a million voters. Put another way, the results indicated that the debates altered the voting behaviour of more than 4% of the electorate. Also, it could be argued that TV coverage of the leaders' debate motivated thousands of voters to use their vote when otherwise they may not have done. In some parts of the country there was a rise of 17% in younger voters indicating that they would turn out to vote. On the other hand, it could be argued that the TV debates only reinforced the existing views most people had.

A third survey from the British Election Study 2010 found 9.4m people watched the first live debate on ITV, 4.5m watched the second debate on Sky and 8.5m the final debate on the BBC. After the second debate, polling figures suggested Cameron and Clegg were joint winners. After the third debate, polling figures suggested Cameron was the winner. Overall, the results from this study appeared to suggest 12% of voters changed their mind about which party to vote for as a consequence of watching the TV election debates.

After the polling stations closed and the votes were counted, it was found that no one party had an overall majority in the House of Commons. The Conservatives obtained the largest share of the overall vote polling 36% (up 3.7% from 2005), Labour attracted 29% of the vote (down 6.2% from 2005) and the Liberal Democrats 23% (up 1% from 2005).

(Adapted from various sources)

Source A is a written source and the title suggests it will give us information about the televised debates.

Source A has been adapted from various sources. The sources are mentioned in the text.

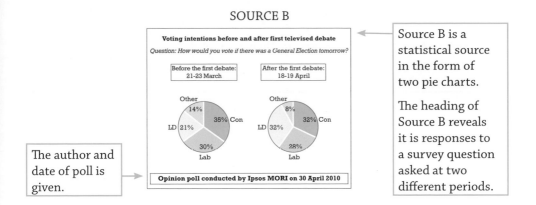

SOURCE B

Source B is a statistical source in the form of two pie charts.

The heading of Source B reveals it is responses to a survey question asked at two different periods.

The author and date of poll is given.

Attempt the following question, using only the information in Sources A and B opposite and above.

Read the question first. The issue is the significance of TV debates on voting intentions.

To what extent is it accurate to state that the televised debates had a significant impact on voting intentions?

In your answer, you may wish to evaluate the reliability of the sources.

Now you have scanned the sources and identified the instruction and issue from the question, you must look to extract relevant information. Remember to **synthesise** – link up information from different sources. The statistical source shows two sets of data for different dates. When reading Source A look for information which relates to the results shown in Source B.

Question 1

Study Sources A and B below and opposite then attempt the question that follows.

SOURCE A

The 2010 General Election televised debates

The 2010 General Election witnessed the first live television debates between leaders from each of the three main UK parties — Conservatives, Labour and the Liberal Democrats. Cameron, Brown and Clegg all hoped to visually connect with voters during a tightly fought campaign nicknamed the 'digital election'.

Before the first-ever debate of its kind, an Ipsos MORI poll revealed 60% of those voters surveyed felt the TV debates would be important to them in helping decide the way they would vote. The performance of the candidates during the debates could also have the potential to alter the way the media would handle coverage of each of the leaders and their parties. Following the debates, a range of polls suggested Nick Clegg had won convincingly, with many voters indicating they would switch to the Liberal Democrats. The success of Nick Clegg led to claims of 'Cleggmania' and a prediction of a historic increase in the number of seats for the Liberal Democrats.

A second survey conducted after the election by an independent polling organisation found the leaders' TV debates changed the voting intentions of more than a million voters. Put another way, the results indicated that the debates altered the voting behaviour of more than 4% of the electorate. Also, it could be argued that TV coverage of the leaders' debate motivated thousands of voters to use their vote when otherwise they may not have done. In some parts of the country there was a rise of 17% in younger voters indicating that they would turn out to vote. On the other hand, it could be argued that the TV debates only reinforced the existing views most people had.

A third survey from the British Election Study 2010 found 9.4m people watched the first live debate on ITV, 4.5m watched the second debate on Sky and 8.5m the final debate on the BBC. After the second debate, polling figures suggested Cameron and Clegg were joint winners. After the third debate, polling figures suggested Cameron was the winner. Overall, the results from this study appeared to suggest 12% of voters changed their mind about which party to vote for as a consequence of watching the TV election debates.

After the polling stations closed and the votes were counted, it was found that no one party had an overall majority in the House of Commons. The Conservatives obtained the largest share of the overall vote polling 36% (up 3.7% from 2005), Labour attracted 29% of the vote (down 6.2% from 2005) and the Liberal Democrats 23% (up 1% from 2005).

(Adapted from various sources)

SOURCE B

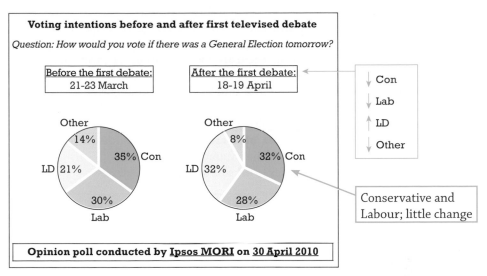

Attempt the following question, using only the information in Sources A and B opposite and above.

To what extent is it accurate to state that the televised debates had a significant impact on voting intentions?

In your answer, you may wish to evaluate the reliability of the sources.

Now you have scanned the sources and identified the instruction and issue from the question, you must look to extract relevant information. Remember to **synthesise** – link up information from different sources. The statistical source shows two sets of data for different dates. When reading Source A look for information which relates to the results shown in Source B.

Creating an answer

SQA principal marking guidelines on 8-mark source-based objectivity questions:

- **Up to 6 marks** are available for the **accurate evaluation** of the given view using evidence.
- Candidates may also be credited up to **2 marks** on any comment/analysis of the **origin and reliability of the sources**, although this is not mandatory.
- **Up to 2 marks** are available for an **overall judgement** as to the extent of accuracy/ objectivity of the view. A **maximum of 6 marks** will be awarded if **no overall judgement** is made on the extent of the accuracy of the statement.
- For full marks candidates must refer to **all** sources in their answer.

Once you have read the sources and identified relevant information, you must group this information together to ensure you synthesise the sources. Decide which information supports the view and which opposes it. You may not need to use all the evidence you have identified in order to gain full marks, there is plenty of information to choose from. You must ensure you highlight where the statement has been accurate and inaccurate and provide evidence from the sources to show this.

Example paragraph to show the statement to be accurate

The statement is accurate as Source A states that an independent polling organisation found the leaders' TV debates changed the voting intentions of more than a million voters. Synthesis Source B shows that after the first debate more people wanted to vote for the Liberal Democrats than before the TV debate. Judgement This shows the statement to be accurate.

This paragraph would score **1 mark** because:

   ✓   Appropriate evidence has been selected from Source A.
   ✗   No figures have been taken from Source B to prove the point further.
   ✗   The point has not been developed enough to be awarded more marks.

This is a better paragraph:

The statement is accurate as Source A states that an independent polling organisation found the leaders' TV debates changed the voting intentions of more than a million voters, which is 4% of the electorate. Synthesis Source B shows that prior to the first debate the Conservatives were in the lead in the polls. However, after the first debate the Liberal Democrats increased their points by 11% and were joint first in the poll with the Conservatives. Judgement This shows that the debate had an impact on the voting intentions of the 9.4 million people who watched it.

This answer would score **2 marks** because:

> ✓   Appropriate evidence has been selected from Source A.
> ✓   Evidence has been synthesised between Sources A and B.
> ✓   Statistics have been selected to help form a judgement.
> ✓   Evidence has been linked back to the statement from the question and a judgement has been made to show the statement to be accurate.

Another possible paragraph to show the statement to be accurate:

Source A states that a range of polls suggested Nick Clegg has won the TV debates convincingly and his popularity increased. Synthesis Evidence from the Ipsos MORI poll (Source B) shows the Liberal Democrats to have increased their popularity the most after the first TV debate. After the first debate the Conservatives lost 3%, Labour lost 2% and Others lost 6%, whereas the

Liberal Democrats increased by 11%, the only party to see an increase in the polls. Judgement Therefore, evidence shows the first TV debate had a significant impact on the voting intentions of those who were originally voting for Others and the Liberal Democrats. It had little impact on those intending to vote Labour or Conservative.

This paragraph would score **3 marks** because:

> ✓   Appropriate evidence has been selected from Source A.
> ✓   Evidence has been synthesised between Sources A and B.
> ✓   Statistics have been selected to help form a judgement.
> ✓   Evidence has been linked back to the statement from the question, and an insightful judgement has been made to show the extent of the accuracy of the statement.

A possible paragraph to show the statement to be inaccurate:

Judgement The televised debate did not have a significant impact on voting intentions since Synthesis the poll conducted before and after the first TV debate (Source B) shows the Labour and Conservative vote to be largely unchanged.

This paragraph would score **1 mark** because:

> ✓   Appropriate evidence has been selected from Source B.
> ✗   No figures have been taken from Source B to prove the point further.
> ✗   The point has not been developed enough to be awarded more marks.

Another possible paragraph to show the statement to be inaccurate:

Results from the British Election Study (Source A) suggest 12% of voters changed their minds about which party to vote for as a consequence of watching the TV election debates. Synthesis *However, a poll by Ipsos MORI (Source B) shows very little change in the percentages for Labour and Conservatives of voters who said they would vote for them. Before the first TV debate 35% claimed to vote Conservative, this decreased to 32% after the debate. Similarly, 30% of people said they would vote Labour before the debate but only 28% after.* Judgement *Therefore, the TV debates did not have a significant impact.*

This paragraph would score **2 marks** because:

> ✓ Appropriate evidence has been selected from Source A.
> ✓ Evidence has been synthesised between Sources A and B.
> ✓ Evidence has been linked to the statement from the question and a judgement has been made.

Another possible paragraph to show the statement to be inaccurate:

Source A states the TV debates helped turn the 2010 election into a 'digital election'. Synthesis *A number of polls suggested Nick Clegg won the debates convincingly with many people saying they would switch their vote to the Liberal Democrats.* Synthesis *This led to claims of 'Cleggmania' in which the Liberal Democrats were predicted to do very well in the election.* Judgement *However, this did not turn out to be the case.* Synthesis *The Liberal Democrats increased their vote by only 1% from the previous election in 2005.* Judgement *Therefore, it is fair to say that the TV debates did not have a significant impact on voting intentions. Although Nick Clegg enjoyed much popularity from the debate performances, the votes for the Liberals did not differ from their previous election performances.*

This paragraph would score **3 marks** because:

> ✓ Appropriate evidence has been selected from Source A.
> ✓ Evidence has been synthesised within Source A.
> ✓ The evidence has been linked back to the statement from the question.
> ✓ An insightful judgement has been made and developed as to the accuracy of the statement.

Example commentaries on the reliability of the sources

Example 1:

Source A contains a variety of sources including polls from Ipsos MORI, the British Election Study and an independent company survey. The information in Source A has been adapted, the extent to which and for what purposes is unknown. This could suggest the information has been specifically selected. Therefore, as a whole, Source A is not entirely reliable.

Example 2:

Information from Ipsos MORI has been used in both sources. Ipsos MORI are an independent research company who always provide election analysis. The information in Source B provides the survey question and the dates the survey was carried out. However Source B does not provide the sample size, so we do not know how many people took part in the poll. Source B is however more reliable than Source A.

Each would score the available **2 marks** because:

> ✓ The authorship of the source has been clarified i.e. an independent research company.
> ✓ An explanation as to why the source is limited has been included.
> ✓ A judgement on the reliability of the source has been made.

An overall judgement on the extent of accuracy of the statement

When providing an overall judgement it is important to try to avoid repeating the same information you have already stated. Evaluate the answers you have given and decide if the statement is correct or incorrect.

Judgement Overall, the evidence does not support the view that the TV debates made a significant impact on voting intentions. Source 1 shows the final results of the 2010 election. The Conservatives won 36% of the vote, Labour won 29% and the Liberal Democrats 23% (only 1% more than 2005 despite Cleggmania). Synthesis These figures do not differ much from those in the poll before the first TV debate. The Conservatives polled at 35%, Labour at 30% and Liberal Democrats 21%. Judgement Therefore, it is inaccurate to suggest a significant impact was had.

This overall judgement would score **2 marks** because:

> ✓ Appropriate evidence has been selected from Source A.
> ✓ Evidence has been synthesised with Source B.
> ✓ The evidence is relevant to the statement.
> ✓ An overall judgement has been made.

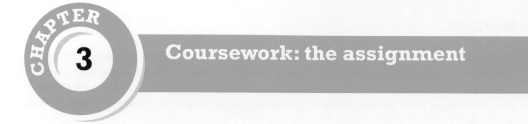

Coursework: the assignment

As part of your overall grade you will complete coursework prior to the final exam in May. The coursework is in the form of an assignment. You will decide your own issue which you will research. You will then gather your findings, form an argument and cite sources. Your assignment will be written under **controlled conditions** (1 hour 30 minutes) in your school and sent to the SQA to be marked. Remember the assignment is worth 30 marks and the question paper is worth 60 marks. The coursework accounts for one third of your final grade. Therefore it is important you spend time and effort on this.

The SQA General Assessment Information states:

Candidates should choose an area of study which allows them to analyse a complex **contemporary issue and apply decision making skills**. They should research the issue, **analyse, evaluate and synthesise information**, show detailed knowledge and understanding of the issue, **reach a decision while showing an awareness of alternatives**, and **communicate information using the conventions of a report. Candidates should use the specified resources (Research Evidence) collected during their research to support them in the production of evidence stage.**

What this means:

You need to choose to research a modern and up-to-date issue in which there are arguments in support and against and/or alternative options. You must be able to make a judgement yourself based on your research.

You must use your higher-order thinking skills and examine the issue in detail, make a judgement on what the evidence shows and link evidence from one source to another. In other words, show when one source of information backs up or contradicts another.

Based on your evidence create a line of argument but also show your awareness that not everyone will agree with you so offer another solution or proposal.

Your assignment will be written in the style of a report which means it must include detailed headings.

When you are writing your report under exam conditions you will be able to refer to a pre-written source sheet. You must refer to these sources at relevant points in your report. You MUST NOT copy information from your resource sheet.

In summary, there are six steps to follow that will help you carry out your research and produce your evidence in the style of a report:

Six steps to assignment success

Step 1: Decide which area of study you are most interested in.
Step 2: Consider a relevant and contemporary issue.
Step 3: Research the issue for information.
Step 4: Make a decision as to your line of argument.
Step 5: Consider an alternative option.
Step 6: Present your findings in the style of a report.

Step 1: Decide which area of study you are most interested in. Choose from:

- Democracy in Scotland and the United Kingdom
- Social Inequality in the United Kingdom
- Crime and the Law in the United Kingdom
- World Powers
- World Issues

Your assignment does not necessarily have to be about an issue you studied in class, as you have an open choice, but it should be an issue you already have some knowledge or awareness about. For example, you may have studied Social Inequality in the United Kingdom as part of the course but you could choose an assignment topic that focuses on Crime and the Law.

Step 2: Consider a relevant and contemporary issue. Once you have decided the area of study you must consider a relevant and contemporary issue. It must therefore be up-to-date and topical. Perhaps an issue which is quite controversial that will help you establish convincing arguments and counter-arguments.

The Higher Modern Studies Course Notes textbook contains assignment ideas in each chapter. Below are some more ideas. This list is by no means exhaustive, but it gives you an idea of the acceptable and appropriate areas of research. Your research should be put forward in the form of a proposal.

- Scotland should/should not be an independent country.
- 16 and 17-year-olds should/should not be allowed to vote in General and Scottish Parliament elections.
- Trident should/should not remain in Scotland.
- The UK should/should not have nuclear weapons.
- The First Past the Post system at Westminster should be replaced by a proportional representation system.

- Voters should be able to vote online in elections.
- Voting in elections should be made compulsory for all eligible citizens.
- MPs that represent Scottish constituencies should not be allowed to vote on matters which affect English and Welsh constituencies only.
- The House of Lords should be abolished.
- Britain should leave the European Union.
- Free school meals should be available for all primary and secondary school pupils.
- People in Scotland should pay for their prescriptions.
- The NHS should introduce a consultation charge for a visit to the GP.
- The NHS should charge people for an overnight stay in hospital.
- The age to buy cigarettes should be increased to 21.
- E-cigarettes should be banned.
- Free childcare should be available until children leave primary school.
- The state pension should be means-tested.
- Positive discrimination for disadvantaged students should be introduced for entry into higher education.
- Benefit claimants should be given vouchers to buy necessities instead of money.
- Energy prices should be regulated by the state.
- Fox hunting should/should not be legal anywhere in the UK.
- Cannabis should be legalised in the UK.
- Sobriety bracelets should be introduced in the UK.
- The main focus of prisons should be punishment.
- Prisoners should be allowed to vote in elections.
- In order to rehabilitate, prisoners should be allowed to access the internet.
- Police in Britain should be armed.
- The 'Not Proven' verdict should be abolished in Scotland.
- The age of criminal responsibility in Scotland should be increased/decreased.
- Sex offenders should be held in one prison establishment.
- Assisted suicide should be decriminalised in Scotland and/or the UK.
- Air weapons should not have to be licensed.
- Capital punishment is an abuse of human rights and should be abolished.
- The Affordable Care Act in the USA should be repealed.
- The second amendment in the American Constitution should be repealed.
- Russia should be allowed to retain Crimea.
- UK/international foreign aid should be increased.
- Trade barriers faced by African sellers in Europe should be lifted.

Step 3: Begin your research. Note down the source of all your information as you go along. This will save you vital time when you come to write your findings. You could refer to your Resource Sheet as shown earlier in the book. This may save you time in identifying sources you have already read or seen on your issue. Remember to use the skills you have learned from the skills-based questions by drawing conclusions from your chosen sources and considering their reliability.

It is important you recognise a good source of information – one that is factual and not the opinion of someone else. You should use official websites and publications only. Blogs can be referred to if analysing public opinion. You must also remember to check the publication date to ensure it is not too old.

A good researcher will conduct **primary and secondary research**. Primary research is any type of research that you go out and collect yourself. Examples include surveys, interviews, observations, emails, focus groups or letters.

Conducting primary research is a useful skill to acquire as it can greatly supplement your research from secondary sources, such as websites, books or TV programmes.

Primary sources	Secondary sources
Conduct a survey to gain people's opinion on your issue. Websites such as surveymonkey.com and debate.org allow you to create your own survey or poll. You can then send the link to your friends or post on social media, which will allow you to gain more respondents. The higher the number of respondents the more reliable the survey or poll will be.	**Data analysis of official statistics**. Official statistics are gathered by professional statisticians who are experts in their field. The data is easily obtained, either by accessing a government website or sending a Freedom of Information Request for the particular data you are looking for. Official statistics are up to date and published on a regular basis. It may sometimes appear that the statistics are out of date, but bear in mind it can take months to gather, analyse and publish the data. For example, you may be carrying out your research in 2016 but the most recent statistics will be dated 2014. Remember the research may have been carried out or presented with a political agenda in mind. Note: The Freedom of Information Act allows members of the public to make a request for information and data held by public agencies.
Organise a focus group to ask the views and opinions of those who would be affected by your proposal. This is different from a survey because it allows the group of people to hold a discussion about it and exchange their views with one another.	**The internet** hosts a variety of secondary sources including news articles, websites of government agencies, international organisations, pressure groups and charities. Again, bear in mind the website may be biased and have a particular

Primary sources	Secondary sources
For example, you could ask a group of parents their thoughts about free childcare or school meals; or a group of farmers about Britain's exit from EU; or various groups of people of similar ages about their thoughts on the legalisation of cannabis, then compare the opinions of each group. Make sure you record or note the main points from the discussions and be prepared to lead the discussions by asking open questions and follow-up questions.	agenda. Website domains which end in .org or .gov.uk are trustworthy as they are usually the domain address for government agencies and organisations that carry out research. Other domain addresses could be websites set up by individuals so the information could be biased or unreliable.
Visit and observe a working environment associated with your research e.g. a prison, jobcentre, Parliament. This will give you a valuable insight and help you to better understand the issues surrounding your proposal.	**TV documentaries** can be very useful and contain information and interviews from a variety of sources. However bear in mind the documentary may be biased and seek to present a particular viewpoint.
Conduct a structured interview with someone who has experience of your particular area of study e.g. a police officer, social worker, farmer, politician, teacher or academic, lawyer, NHS worker etc. This will allow you to hear informed views and opinions from someone who works in the field.	**Academic reading** of official reports and publications including textbooks will provide in-depth knowledge written by professional researchers.
Send an email or a letter if you cannot arrange to interview a particular person. Perhaps their job is too demanding to give you the time or they may live and work far away. Make sure your email/letter is clear in your intentions and contains appropriate open questions that allow for the person to expand on their answers. Detail the ways in which the recipient can contact you.	**Social media** provides an insight into public opinion on some topical news issues, but remember the views expressed by some on social media do not represent the views of all.

Word bank

Closed question: a question that requires a 'Yes' or 'No' response, e.g. Do you think Scotland should be an independent country?

Data: information or facts.

Open question: a question which requires a detailed answer and cannot be answered by one word. Open questions usually start with Who, What, Why, When, Where or How. For example, 'Why do you think the British police force should be armed with guns?' 'Where in the UK should nuclear weapons be kept if not in Scotland?' 'Who should be responsible for informing schools of a parent's imprisonment?' 'What actions should the UK government take against ISIS?'

Statistic: a fact in the form of a number that gives information about something.

Statistician: someone who studies statistics and uses numbers to present information.

Structured interview: an interview for which you have prepared your questions before you go.

Sources of information

It is important you know where to look for good quality, reliable secondary sources. The internet is a good place to start, but you must be able to distinguish between fact, opinion, bias and exaggeration because there are many websites which contain inaccurate and biased information. You should aim to use official figures or publications. The sources detailed below should give you a starting point but are by no means the only sources available to research. Remember, if a website does not show the information you are looking for you can always carry out a Freedom of Information request or email/telephone for more information.

Word bank

Freedom of Information request: a request for information under the Freedom of Information Act, which gives people the right to access recorded information held by public organisations.

Independent research companies

Ipsos MORI is a well-known UK research company which carries out social and political research on behalf of others. In particular it conducts election polls to give an indication of voting intentions before an election and voting patterns once the election has been concluded. The Political and Social Trends section of the website is very useful and contains up-to-date information about voting patterns, views of political parties as well as many social issues such as immigration and the NHS. The research is presented as PDF publications containing text, images and statistical diagrams.

Lord Ashcroft Polls is another useful source for social and political research. Publications include election analysis as well as public opinion about key political and social issues, including the 2014 Independence Referendum.

YouGov is a recognised public opinion forum with millions of members providing their opinions on a vast range of political, social, economic and international issues. YouGov then publishes a selection of findings on its website. There is a search function on the website.

ScotCen Social Research is an independent research agency which conducts social research on behalf of government and charities. You can easily search the website for anything related to your topic of research.

Democracy in Scotland and the United Kingdom

Education Scotland (political literacy) http://www.educationscotland.gov.uk/resources/c/genericresource_tcm4813895.asp This webpage is useful in providing clarification and explanation on some key political arrangements. This webpage will give you information about: Scotland's independence referendum; an explanation of key political terms and institutions; details about the rights of young people and women; and the power of social media in the political world.

For information on current legislation, debates and members you can refer to the websites of the **Scottish** and **UK Parliaments**.

Each political party has its own website detailing its leader, MSPs/MPs and policies. **The Electoral Reform Society** is an independent organisation which seeks to protect the rights of voters and campaigns for a more democratic Britain. It is well established and carries out extensive research into political systems and arrangements.

The 2014 Scottish Independence Referendum saw the internet turn into a political battleground for both sides. The Yes campaign and the Better Together campaign both had websites which have since been suspended. However, other sources provide useful information. **John Curtice**, Professor of Politics at Strathclyde University, has provided commentary on the referendum and opinion polls on the **What Scotland Thinks** website.

The **BBC** is a useful news source since it is unbiased and does not support any particular political party, unlike newspapers. Its news website contains news stories about UK politics and Scottish politics.

Social Issues

Scottish Government statistics

If your proposal is concerned with Social Inequality in the UK or Crime and the Law in the UK then the Scottish Government website is a good place to start.

The Labour Market section includes details of employment and unemployment figures for Scotland.

The Crime and Justice section contains information about victimisation, perceptions of crime, violent crime, policing, prison populations and many more.

The Social and Welfare section contains information about poverty and income, Scottish welfare fund information and details on the Scottish Index of Multiple Deprivation (SIMD). The SIMD identifies Scotland's poorest areas.

The Scottish Government publish up-to-date statistics on a range of topics.

You will find the list of indicators which are used in the SIMD to define the poorest areas here.

The Office of National Statistics (ONS) is the UK government department of statistics. On its website there is a search function as well as various links to subject areas such as the Labour Market or Crime and Justice. Some findings may exclude Scotland and be concerned with England and Wales only.

Social Inequality in the UK

Gov.uk is a UK government website which details all the benefits and support available from the Welfare State.

The **Joseph Rowntree Foundation** is an independent organisation which campaigns for social change and carries out research. For example, it publishes a Minimum Income Standard every year in which it advises the minimum amount workers and households should receive in order to afford a sustainable living. You will find information on housing, benefits and various vulnerable groups of society.

Livingwage.org is an initiative campaigning to increase the minimum wage to what is called a living wage. The group carries out research and lobbies government and employers to support their cause.

Shelter Scotland is a frontline charity supporting and campaigning against issues concerned with homelessness, bad housing and rogue landlords.

The Equality and Human Rights Commission is a national human rights institution which aims to promote and protect human rights. You will find information on the Publications and Newsroom parts of its website. You may find information relevant to Crime and Law topics too.

Crime and the Law in the UK

The Scottish Crime and Justice Survey is the official government source of crime. It is a large-scale social survey which conducts face-to-face interviews with randomly selected adults about their experiences and perceptions of crime. The sample size is around 6000 adults each year. The survey is carried out by independent research companies on behalf of the Scottish government. Data from this survey is used to shape and drive Scottish government policy.

The Crime Survey for England and Wales (previously known as the British Crime Survey) is carried out on an annual basis. Face-to-face interviews are conducted with around 35,000 adults and 3000 children. The participants are asked about their experiences and perceptions of crime. Data from this survey is used to shape and drive UK government policy.

The Scottish Prison Service (SPS) website details types of prisons, location and visiting times of all Scottish prisons. Contact details of each prison are shown which can be used if you wish to carry out primary research.

HMIP Inspection Reports. Prisons are routinely inspected by Her Majesty's Inspectorate of Prisons who visit prisons to ensure they are achieving their aims. HMIP publishes its findings and highlights areas of good practice within the prison and/or areas in which the prison is failing the inmates. You will find inspection reports for Scottish prisons on the Scottish government website and English, Welsh and Northern Irish prisons on the UK government website.

Prison Reform Trust is a registered charity which works to create an effective and just penal system in the UK. It carries out extensive research in prisons and releases its publications on its website.

Families Outside is a charity supporting the families and children of prisoners. It carries out research and publishes its work on its website.

Inside Time is the national newspaper for prisoners. It contains information about the prison regimes of most UK prisons, current headline news stories and letters from inmates.

UK national newspapers

Newspapers are useful sources of information because they contain up-to-date information and are published on a daily basis. Newspapers will report on issues in relation to democracy, social issues, crime and law as well as international countries and issues too. Many newspapers have online versions or apps which help to access important stories. Newspapers are also useful to gauge public opinion and mood about particular issues, since newspapers will print what their readers want to read about and can sensationalise headlines. There is a letters page in which people can write to the newspaper with their comments about news stories. Readers can also leave their comments online on the newspaper's Facebook or Twitter accounts.

However, be very careful when using articles from newspapers because they could be biased. Newspapers can choose to support a political party and print biased stories and headlines in favour of their chosen party. For example, the Scottish Sun backed Nicola Sturgeon and the SNP during the 2015 General Election campaign. Depending on its loyalties, a newspaper can be critical or supportive of government policies and new legislation. This can therefore influence public opinion to a certain extent.

There are two different types of newspaper between which you must be able to distinguish: broadsheets and tabloids.

Word bank

Broadsheet: a newspaper that was traditionally printed on large sheets of paper (some have downsized in recent years). Broadsheet newspapers are considered to provide more serious journalism than tabloid newspapers.

Tabloid: a popular newspaper smaller in size than a broadsheet. Tabloids contain short, easy to read reports with many pictures.

Newspaper	Type	Support in 2015 General Election
The Telegraph	Broadsheet	Conservatives
The Times	Broadsheet	Conservatives
The Financial Times	Broadsheet	Conservative & Lib Dem Coalition
The Guardian	Broadsheet	Labour
The Observer	Broadsheet	Labour
The Independent	Broadsheet	Conservative & Lib Dem Coalition
Daily Mail	Tabloid	Conservatives
Daily Express	Tabloid	UKIP
Mail on Sunday	Tabloid	Conservatives
The Sun	Tabloid	Conservatives; SNP in Scotland
Daily Mirror	Tabloid	Labour

Pressure groups

UK pressure groups campaign to governments for change on a whole host of issues. Below are only a few examples of the many pressure groups operating in the UK.

The **Scottish Campaign for Nuclear Disarmament** is a group which campaigns against nuclear weapons held at Faslane in Scotland. Its website provides information about its campaign and its arguments against nuclear weapons.

Friends of the Earth is a pressure group which campaigns about environmental issues such as fracking. Its website contains details about its most recent campaigns as well as information about environmental issues at home and abroad (including African land grabs) and the EU's impact on environmental issues in Britain.

Word bank

Fracking: this is short for hydraulic fracturing, a process of extracting oil and gas. The process involves creating cracks in the rock under the surface which allow the oil and gas to escape. This is a controversial method as many argue it damages the environment and causes earthquakes.

Greenpeace is a large well-known international pressure group which campaigns about environmental issues such as fracking and oil exploitation.

The Countryside Alliance is a pressure group which campaigns about UK rural affairs.

Save the Children is a large charity which works and campaigns against poverty in the UK and abroad.

Christian Aid is an international development agency which works in the UK and abroad.

SCIAF is the Scottish Catholic International Aid Fund which is an international development agency. It carries out work in the UK and abroad.

Amnesty International is a non-governmental agency which conducts research and campaigns for human rights worldwide in accordance with international law.

International Issues – World Powers

The USA

The **Pew Research Centre** is an independent American think-tank which carries out social science research in regard to public opinion, social issues and demographic trends. Its work is highly regarded. You can search for information on its website via the Publications section or Topics section.

The National Rifle Association (NRA) is your go-to source for arguments in favour of gun rights. With over 5 million members, including some notable celebrities, the NRA lobbies government and campaigns to protect gun rights.

Various media outlets will provide current headline news stories and can be a measure of public opinion in America. These include **CNN Politics**, **USA Today, Fox News and Democracy Now!** but there are many more.

Europe

The **European Parliament** website is a good place to start for issues concerning European countries and the EU. You can also find and contact your MEP.

Open Europe is an independent policy think-tank which provides information and views on current European affairs. It publishes articles about various topics including immigration, trade, the Eurozone, Britain in the EU and more. It also publishes a weekly opinion poll on its website.

China

Media outlets including **China Today** provide up-to-date news stories, as well as **Al-Jazeera, Reuters** and the **BBC News** websites which will also cover Chinese news stories.

International Issues – World Issues

Developmental issues

The **UN website** is a good place to start. Here you will find information on the most current issues concerning the UN as well as links to the websites of the various UN agencies, including the **World Health Organisation (WHO), World Food Programme (WFP), Food and Agriculture Organisation (FAO), International Fund for Agricultural Development (IFAD), United Nations Children's Emergency Fund (UNICEF), International Labour Organisation (ILO), International Monetary Fund (IMF),** and the **United Nations Educational, Scientific and Cultural Organisation (UNESCO).** The websites of each UN agency will have details of publications and recent data.

The **World Bank** publishes development reports on a range of issues on its website.

The UK government's **Department for International Development (DfID)** provides information and publications about the UK's work and contribution to international development including the UK's international assistance budget.

The Woodrow Wilson International Center for Scholars is a world-renowned US think-tank which researches and publishes information and views on various international issues.

Roll Back Malaria provides information on the global fight against malaria. Its website includes fact sheets and statistics.

One World is a UK-based charity which works to provide mobile and web technologies in third-world countries. Its website details the work it does in regard to promoting technology, democracy and women's rights, as well as facts, statistics and publications.

Research skills

Reading for information

Reading for information is a useful skill which will help you to read, understand and retain as well as ensure you are using your time well by reading relevant information.

Firstly, scan the page(s) for hints to show what information is included in the text. The hints are in the form of:

- The **title** and **sub-headings** are usually in a bolder or larger font and will stand out from the main text. These will inform you what the text is about and the various sections discussed in the text.
- The **introduction** will set out the main ideas.
- The **first sentence** of each paragraph will state what the paragraph will be about.
- **Bold** or italic font is used for important information.
- **Bullet pointed** text summarises key information.
- **Charts, graphs, diagrams** and **tables** provide a pictorial representation of important information.

Clarification in the difference between absolute and relative poverty. The bullet points help to make this stand out.

This section of the report provides an overview of poverty across the UK. The rest of the report goes into more detail.

The information has been organised into paragraphs. Key words in each sentence tell the reader what information that paragraph contains.

Summary

This note sets out information on the levels and rates of poverty in the UK, including historical trends and forecasts for future years. The focus here is on poverty defined in terms of disposable household income, although poverty may be defined in different ways and there is no single, universally accepted definition.

Various poverty measures based on disposable household income are in common use and the trend can look quite different depending on the measure used. Two commonly used measures are:

- people in relative low income – living in households with income below 60% of the median in that year;
- people in absolute low income – living in households with income below 60% of (inflation-adjusted) median income in some base year, usually 2010/11.

So the 'relative low income' measure compares households against the rest of the population in that year, while the 'absolute low income' measure looks at whether living standards at the bottom of the distribution are improving over time. A low income measure can also be combined with an assessment of whether households have access to key goods and services, for a measure of low income and material deprivation.

Income can be measured before or after housing costs are deducted (BHC or AHC). Poverty levels tend to be higher based on income measured after housing costs, because poorer households tend to spend a higher proportion of their income on housing.

Over the longer-term, there has been a reduction in poverty rates since the late 1990s for children, pensioners and working-age parents, although the likelihood of being in relative low income has increased for working-age adults without dependent children.

Poverty levels in the UK, 2014/15: all individuals

		Number of people	Change on year	% of population
Relative low income	BHC	10.1 million	up 500,000	16%
	AHC	13.5 million	up 300,000	21%
Absolute low income	BHC	9.4 million	down 500,000	15%
	AHC	12.9 million	down 700,000	20%

Poverty levels in the UK, 2014/15: children

		Number of children	Change on year	% of all children
Relative low income	BHC	2.5 million	up 200,000	19%
	AHC	3.9 million	up 200,000	29%
Absolute low income	BHC	2.3 million	unchanged	17%
	AHC	3.7 million	down 100,000	27%
Low income and material deprivation		1.7 million	unchanged	13%

The Institute for Fiscal Studies estimates that the number of people in relative low income will stay roughly unchanged up to 2015/16, after which it is projected to increase. The share of people in relative low income is projected to be around 18% in 2020/21, the same as in 2007/08. The rate of absolute low income on the other hand is expected to have fallen between 2013/14 and 2015/16 and is then projected to stay flat to 2020/21.

Although this note discusses income-based measures of poverty, these have been criticised by the current Government as failing to acknowledge the root causes of poverty and resulting in skewed policy responses that try to lift those just below the poverty threshold to just above it. For further background, see the Library's briefing paper prepared for Second Reading of the Welfare Reform and Work Bill.

Another source of information, The Institute of Fiscal Studies is referenced here.

Key information on poverty across the UK for individuals and children are shown in graphs. The shows that overall poverty and child poverty are important issues.

Separating fact from opinion

Facts cannot be disputed, whereas opinion can. Look at the newspaper article below which highlights the difference between fact and opinion:

What Better Together learned too late

Yes Scotland's relationship with the Scottish National Party government in Edinburgh has been far too close. Their attempts to make the argument for Yes into a cross-party affair failed. In the final weeks of the campaign, Yes Scotland disappeared from the airwaves almost entirely, as SNP minister after minister dominated the TV debates (with Patrick Harvie MSP, co-convenor of the Scottish Greens, more or less the only non-SNP Yesser on prominent display). Away from the official Yes Scotland outfit, it is certainly true that the broader Yes movement has been cross-party, but that has had much more to do with the plethora of unofficial grass-roots groups (Women for Independence, National Collective, Common Weal, Bella Caledonia, etc) than it has had to do with the Yes Scotland leader, Blair Jenkins, and his team on Hope Street.

Only 200 metres away, on another of the main arteries in Glasgow city centre, Sauchiehall Street, are the headquarters of Better Together. They have had to bear a far greater load than their counterparts in Yes Scotland, for two reasons. First, the government backing them was 400 miles away and led by English Tories. And second, the No side of the argument never produced anything close to the range of grass-roots groups that so galvanised, energised and, indeed, mobilised the campaign for independence.

There are some things Better Together did brilliantly and some others where, as they say, lessons may be learned. Let's do the opposite of how the campaign was so often perceived, and start with the positives. First, it should never be overlooked just how unusual a beast in British politics was the Better Together campaign. Even in this era of coalition government in London, can there have been co-operation in peacetime between Conservatives, Labour and Liberal Democrats of the kind we have seen here? Of course it has sometimes been rough. There have been disagreements along the way. Yet these have occurred as much within the parties as between them. When it was stormy, the calm authority of Alistair Darling anchored the campaign. He may not be the most florid orator, but he has a steady determination and no little steel and, in private, he shows warmth and remarkable generosity. There are few in the No camp more deserving of our admiration than he, whatever the result.

The nearer we got to polling day, the less the campaign became about statehood and the more it became about policy, from child poverty to social justice, from Gaza to Iraq, and from health service 'privatisation' to the bedroom tax and welfare reform. The idea of Yes became a rhetorical vessel into which you could pour all your hopes and aspirations, all your fears and frustrations. What do you want? Vote Yes and you can have it. What's wrong? Vote Yes and it will go away.

Fact:

✓ Most politicians championing Scottish independence in the media were SNP members apart from Patrick Harvie.
✓ Many grass-root groups showed support for Scottish independence.
✓ The headquarters of both campaigns were in Glasgow.
✓ The Better Together campaign was led by a government in London.
✓ The Better Together campaign had little grass-root support.
✓ Representatives from both sides stated their policies on issues important to the electorate.

Opinion:

✓ The relationship between Yes Scotland and the SNP was 'too close'.
✓ The Better Together campaign had 'a far greater load to bear'.
✓ The Better Together campaign performed 'brilliantly'.
✓ The rhetorical question suggests a viewpoint.
✓ Complimentary characteristics of the Better Together leader.
✓ People poured their emotions into the Yes campaign.

Source: *http://www.newstatesman.com/politics/2014/09/what-better-to-gether-learned-too-late*

Synthesising sources

How do I synthesise the sources?

A key element of what you are expected to produce in your final assignment is synthesis of sources. This means finding information from different sources which agree or contradict one another. This shows the examiner you have carried out detailed research and have considered a variety of sources in your evaluation of the argument you are expressing. Therefore, as you conduct your research, look for similarities or differences between sources and take note of them. If you find a valid argument in one source, find a statistic from another reliable source to support this.

Step 4: Using the information from your research and/or class notes make a decision as to your line of argument.

When you decide your assignment issue and word it in the form of a proposal as the previous examples show, you may already have an idea about your own opinion and whether you are in favour or against your proposal. You must bear in mind that the assignment is not concerned with your own personal opinion. Instead, the task is for you to research and consider evidence and argue a point of view based on this evidence. Therefore, it is important you have enough information to provide a clear line of argument. You must also show the arguments opponents to your proposal may put forward. These arguments must then be rebutted. This means you need to outline what the arguments against your proposal are, then show that they are invalid and your proposal is still the appropriate course of action. In other words, you answer back the arguments against by knocking them down!

Step 5: Consider an alternative option to the one you are proposing in relation to the issue.

Once you have outlined your arguments in favour of your proposal, the ones against and rebutted these then you must concede an alternative option. This does not mean a different proposal altogether, but instead another option. In order to achieve the full 30 marks available candidates must present at least two alternative options. For example, your proposal could be to legalise marijuana in the UK. An alternative option could be to give GPs the power to prescribe marijuana on medical grounds instead of legalising it completely for everyone. A second alternative could be to introduce on-the-spot fines for those in possession in order to prevent users obtaining a criminal record.

Step 6: Produce your findings and present them in the style of a report.

Your assignment must be presented in the style of a report. You can be awarded up to 4 marks for appropriate formatting, so you must ensure you include headings (otherwise it will be in an essay style which is inappropriate), an introduction, a clear recommendation and a conclusion. You must also evaluate the usefulness and reliability of a range of sources of information. The SQA have not specified the headings you should include, therefore it is your choice how you present your arguments and evidence. However, an example structure is provided on page 122.

Assignment mark allocation: advice from the SQA

In presenting their findings, candidates should show the following skills, knowledge and understanding:

Criteria	Mark allocation	What this means
A. Identifying and demonstrating knowledge and understanding of the issue about which a decision is to be made, including alternative courses of action.	A maximum of 10 marks are available. 5 knowledge marks are available for background information and 5 are available for knowledge that backs up analysis.	The first 5 knowledge marks can be gained in your introduction if the information is relevant and is used to show the significance to the issue in question. To gain full marks you should refer to the political, social, economic and/or international impact of your proposal. You must also provide detail of the two alternative courses of action if your proposal is denied. Remember one alternative could be to continue with the status quo (no change). The other 5 knowledge marks can be gained through your analysis of your research evidence. This is the knowledge you use to argue your proposal – the facts, figures, quotes you have detailed on your Resource Sheet. Remember, this must not be copied directly from your Resource Sheet.
B. Analysing and synthesising information from a range of sources including use of specified resources.	A maximum of 10 marks are available. In order to gain full analysis marks you MUST refer to more than 3 sources on your Resource Sheet.	You need to use evidence from a source or knowledge to identify an idea or argument by showing: • links between different ideas or arguments • similarities or contradictions in your evidence • consistency or inconsistency in ideas, arguments or evidence • different views or interpretations of your argument • the possible consequence or implication of your proposal/rejection of your proposal • synthesis of sources throughout.

Criteria	Mark allocation	What this means
C. Evaluating the usefulness and reliability of a range of sources of information.	A maximum of 2 marks are available.	In order to gain full marks you must compare the reliability and/or usefulness of at least two sources on your Resource Sheet. Do not evaluate a source which you have not detailed on your sheet.
D. Communicating information using the conventions of a report.	A maximum of 4 marks are available.	To gain the full 4 available marks you need to: • include appropriate headings and sections (see example structure on page 122) • use appropriate social science terminology (see page 9 for specialised Modern Studies vocabulary) • make reference to evidence on your Resource Sheet • present a logical and coherent line of argument throughout.
E. Reaching a decision, supported by evidence, about the issue.	A maximum of 4 marks are available.	You should be clear and confident in your recommendation and show in your report that your chosen course of action is the best. You must use quality researched evidence as shown on your Resource Sheet. You must also explain why you have rejected alternative courses of action.

The Resource Sheet

The SQA advise:

Candidates may take Research Evidence collected during the research phase into the write-up.

This evidence must consist of **no more than two single-sided sheets of A4**. Candidates should be encouraged to briefly annotate or highlight information on their resources before the production of evidence stage.

This Research Evidence must be submitted to the SQA along with the candidate evidence produced during the final production of evidence stage.

The nature of the resources taken into the production of evidence stage may include, for example: evidence/data from primary or secondary research: bullet points/headings; mind maps; statistical, graphical or numerical data; survey results; interview questions and/or answers; questionnaire and/or results; list of internet search engine results; newspaper articles or extracts; summary notes taken from a visit or talk; summary notes taken from a written or audio-visual source.

Beware: what to avoid on your Resource Sheet

✗ You must not copy or paraphrase parts of the information on your Resource Sheet and write this into your report. This is not demonstrating analysis and will not be credited. You can copy quotes for example and statistics and facts but you must do something with the information to be credited analysis marks.

✗ The Resource Sheet has been designed to show the SQA marker the breadth of research you carried out; it is not intended to be a short draft of your assignment.

✗ Do not note your sources on the Resource Sheet in the order you intend to refer to them in your write-up. This will look like a plan and you will not be credited.

✗ All sources should be referenced on the Resource Sheet. The SQA marker will check your sources if they feel they have to.

✗ Resource Sheets which include pre-prepared in-depth analysis of statistical sources may not demonstrate the candidate's own analysis and therefore will not be credited. Instead, the sheet should show the statistics and the analysis should only be shown in the final write-up.

✗ Use information for all the sources shown on your Resource Sheet. Therefore do not have too many. Between six and eight sources should be enough.

You can decide if you want to hand write your resource sheet or word process it. It may be easier to use a computer especially if you have used statistical sources which are then easier to copy and paste or screenshot onto your resource sheet. If you have carried out your own survey you could put the results into a spreadsheet and create statistical graphs and charts which you could then copy to your sheet.

By the time you come to write up your assignment it should be in your memory. You will have had the opportunity to carry out research, draft and re-draft your assignment write-up. However, the SQA have provided strict guidelines to teachers to provide minimal support. The assignment is intended to be a research-based task led by the individual candidate, so teacher help is kept to a minimum. However, there are certainly parts of the report that can be prepared and assigned to memory before you write your report under controlled conditions. For example:

- Your introduction – where **5 knowledge marks** are available.
- Your evaluation of sources – where **2 marks** are available.

- Prepare the structure of your report – where **4 marks** are available.
- Know your decision and reasons for rejecting other proposals – where **4 marks** are available.

The assignment: example structures

The SQA have not provided a set structure they wish all candidates to follow, therefore the examples below are by no means set in stone. Your teacher may guide you on a different structure. Bear in mind this is a report and not an essay, therefore you must include headings. Once you have completed your research, consider the example structures and decide which one suits your information.

Example structure 1

Memo: The topic/problem/issue you have chosen to focus on e.g. Legalisation of Cannabis, Gun Control, Nuclear Weapons, Unemployment, Child Poverty, Penal Policy.

To: For example, the Scottish/UK Government, the US Congress or even a particular person in government such as the Health or Justice Ministers.

Role and remit

Create an advisory role for yourself and state the topic you have researched and what your recommendation is. For example:

I am an advisor to the Health Department and have carried out extensive research into the use of E-cigarettes in public. After careful consideration, I recommend the Scottish Government bans the use of E-cigarettes in all public spaces.

This section is important in setting out your line of argument in a report format. You are making it clear to the examiner that you are not writing an essay and you have stated clearly what your argument is.

Background

Set the scene by detailing what the issue or problem is that needs to be resolved, some relevant facts to show the extent of the problem or issue and put this into the wider context by considering the social, economic, political or international implications of this problem.

For example, if you are recommending that all school children receive a free school meal you could provide some detail about the aims of the welfare state, the extent of child poverty in the UK and its implications on other parts of the welfare state, namely the NHS and education as well as recent changes to other benefits including any popular or unpopular policies. Show the consequences of child poverty and poor diet on the future workforce and welfare state to express the importance of your recommendation. This will show the examiner you have a solid understanding of the importance of the issue and its implications.

This section is important in gaining up to 5 knowledge marks.

Recommendation

State clearly what your recommendation is and outline your three arguments in support. For example you may recommend the introduction of sobriety bracelets to reduce reoffending, or for Britain to become nuclear-free or for the Scottish Parliament to pass the Assisted Suicide Bill.

- Argument 1
- Argument 2
- Argument 3

This section is important in helping you maintain a good structure and coherent argument throughout, which is important in gaining marks for structure.

Reasons to support my recommendation

In this section you should have three separate paragraphs for your three arguments in support of your recommendation. For each argument you should aim to have:

- a point of knowledge
- reference to at least two sources which show consistency or support
- reinforcement of your recommendation following the evidence.

For example:

The UK should become nuclear-free because it is costing the government lots of money to have weapons which they would avoid using at all costs. The cost to employ workers at Trident, maintain, store and carry out nuclear research is considerable. In fact recent research from (Source 5) [state the author/source of the information as shown on your Resource Sheet] states…. This shows…[by explaining the relevance of the information you are developing it further and therefore analysing it. This is where you will gain analysis marks] Furthermore, (Source 2) [state the author/source of information as shown on your Resource Sheet] reinforces/supports/concurs by showing… This therefore means money which could be better spent on other areas of the welfare state, such as the struggling NHS, is needlessly spent on having weapons of mass destruction which the government would not use anyway. [consider the wider social/political/economic implications and refer back to your recommendation to show its importance and relevance.] Therefore, the UK must become nuclear-free in order to redirect vitally needed funds which are currently being used inefficiently.

This section is important in gaining analysis marks. In each argument you should aim to include, in no particular order:

One piece of new background knowledge not mentioned in the Background section and not on your Resource Sheet

Evidence from at least two sources which support each other

Analysis of the evidence

Consideration of your argument in the wider context – social/economic/political/international

Reinforcement of your recommendation at the end

Criticisms of my recommendation

In this section you should note what the opposing arguments are against your proposal and rebut these. This means you bring in new knowledge not previously mentioned to argue against the opposing argument. Remember, you should show the implications of your recommendation in a wider context by considering the political/social/economic and/or international factors. You should show two opposing arguments.

 This section is important to gain analysis and decision marks.

Other courses of action

In this part you should detail two alternative courses of action which could also be of benefit. Some issues do not always allow for two alternatives therefore one can be to remain with the status quo (no change) and review the situation at a later date.

 This section is important to gain analysis and decision marks.

Conclusion

Sum up all your arguments and reinforce your recommendation and its positive impact on social/economic/political and/or international issues.

 This section is important to gain analysis and decision marks.

Methodologies

In this section you must provide an evaluation of your sources and this is worth 2 marks. You can only evaluate sources which you have detailed in your Resource Sheet. In order to gain the full 2 marks you MUST compare at least two of your sources. Consider the sources you found most and least useful and compare with each other. You must also be specific about your sources and not be too general. For example an answer such as:

To research my issue I used the internet which was very useful in providing me with many useful websites to choose from with lots of relevant and up-to-date information. Also, my class notes were very useful as they gave me a starting point and I found lots of information online which backed up my class notes.

Although this statement has attempted to evaluate two sources (the internet and class notes), this answer is too vague and is not what is expected of a Higher candidate. Below are a couple of examples of acceptable responses:

One primary research method I used was to conduct a survey about Scottish Independence. This was useful for gauging public opinion on this matter since the referendum held in September 2014. This method was however limited because my sample size was small (less than 100 people) but it did however allow me to gather the opinions of those in my local community. A larger sample size and the use of SurveyMonkey and social media would have helped me gather the opinions of a wider group of people which would have made the results more reliable.

Another source I used was the SNP's website. Although the website is biased in favour of an independent Scotland this was useful because it allowed me to gather information about the arguments they use to persuade people to support independence. However, I used the facts and statistical information on this website with caution since they may have been manipulated in favour of independence.

The above response shows a good evaluation of two sources and would score **1** out of the **2** available **marks**. The response has given:

> ✓ A clear evaluation of at least one source of evidence as detailed in the Resource Sheet.
> ✓ Generalised statements of the usefulness and reliability of the evidence.

The response failed to achieve the full 2 marks available because:

> ✓ No evaluation making a comparative judgement of at least two sources has been made.

A better response is:

One primary research method I used was to conduct a survey about Scottish Independence. This was useful for gauging public opinion on this matter since the referendum held in September 2014. This method was however limited because my sample size was small (less than 100 people) but it did however allow me to gather the opinions of those in my local community. A larger sample size and the use of SurveyMonkey and social media would have helped me gather the opinions of a wider group of people which would have made the results more reliable. But I was able to compare my survey, albeit small, to the official results of the referendum in 2014 to evaluate a change in public opinion. Also the What Scotland Thinks website was very useful in providing information from various public opinion polls concerning governance, national identity and policy issues which helped me understand the complex issues surrounding the independence debate, which helped to put my own survey results and the referendum results into context. This website is non-partisan and managed by professional researchers and includes comments and analysis from academics and professionals which made it very informative and reliable.

This response would score the full **2** available **marks** because it has made a comparative judgement between at least two sources – the candidate's own survey, the referendum results and opinion polls carried out by professional researchers.

Example structure 2

Memo: The topic/problem/issue you have chosen to focus on e.g. Legalisation of Cannabis, Gun Control, Nuclear Weapons, Unemployment, Child Poverty, Penal Policy.

To: For example, the Scottish/UK Government, the US Congress or even a particular person in government such as the Health or Justice Ministers.

Role and remit

Create an advisory role for yourself and state the topic you have researched and what your recommendation is.

This section is important in setting out your line of argument in a report format. You are making it clear to the examiner that you are not writing an essay and you have stated clearly what your argument is.

Background

Set the scene by detailing what the issue or problem is that needs to be resolved, some relevant facts to show the extent of the problem or issue, and put this into the wider context by considering the social, economic, political or international implications of this problem.

This section is important in gaining up to 5 knowledge marks.

Courses of action

Outline three possible solutions to your topic/issue/problem as outlined in your background section. This section will consist of several paragraphs but will include three main sections, each with a sub-heading of the policy idea. Outline the pros and cons of each policy idea.

For example, if you have researched youth unemployment you may consider three ideas such as scrapping tuition fees, extending voluntary work placements and reforming Jobseeker's Allowance. Or if you have researched reoffending you may consider three ideas such as introducing sobriety bracelets, scrapping short sentences of 6 months or less and investing in rehabilitation programmes in prison.

For each argument you should aim to have:

- a point of knowledge
- reference to at least two sources which show consistency or support.

This section is important in gaining analysis marks. In each argument you should aim to include, in no particular order:

- One piece of new background knowledge not mentioned in the Background section and not on your Resource Sheet.
- Evidence from at least two sources which support each other.
- Analysis of the evidence.
- Consideration of your policy idea in the wider context – social/economic/political/ international.

Report recommendation

Make a final decision by stating clearing the idea you think is the best course of action to deal with the issue/problem/topic. Sum up all your arguments and show how it is better than the alternative ideas. Remember to show its positive impact on social/economic/ political and/or international issues.

This section is important to gain structure and decision marks. 4 decision marks are available.

Methodologies

In this section you must provide an evaluation of your sources and this is worth 2 marks. You can only evaluate sources which you have detailed in your Resource Sheet. In order to gain the full 2 marks you MUST compare at least two of your sources. You must also be specific about your sources and not be too general.

Summary of example structures

Carry out your research on your chosen topic. Evaluate your research evidence and decide which is the best structure for you.

Example structure 1

Memo:

To:

Role and remit

Background

Include 5 points of background knowledge.

Recommendation

Reasons to support my recommendation

Argument 1

Argument 2

Argument 3

This is where you will gain more knowledge marks as well as analysis and decision marks. This section will be the lengthiest part of report.

Criticisms of my recommendation

Include one argument against your proposal.

Other courses of action

A shorter section, detailing one alternative and stating another.

Conclusion

Decision marks are available here.

Methodologies

Worth 2 marks.

Example structure 2

Memo:

To:

Role and remit:

Background

Include 5 points of background knowledge.

Courses of action

Policy idea 1 – pros and cons

Policy idea 2 – pros and cons

Policy idea 3 – pros and cons

This is where you will gain more knowledge marks as well as analysis and decision marks. This section will be the lengthiest part of report.

Report recommendation

Decision marks are available here.

Methodologies

Worth 2 marks.

Remember, it is important your report includes the following (in no particular order):

Assignment Report Checklist

✓ Appropriate headings.
✓ An introduction with 5 points of knowledge and reference to the wider social/ economic/political/international implications of the topic/issue/problem.
✓ An analysis of possible arguments/ideas in reference to your topic/issue/problem.
✓ Consideration of more than one idea.
✓ A convincing and mature argument supported by appropriate and reliable evidence.
✓ Synthesised sources throughout. Reference to only sources which appear on your Resource Sheet.
✓ A clear decision.
✓ A summary of your research methodology.

Preparing for the exam

In order to ensure you are fully prepared for the final Modern Studies examination it is essential you have revised the information effectively. This will allow you to recall the necessary knowledge to answer the extended responses. This section of the book will give you some ideas about how you can go about studying and realising which way is the most effective for you.

Firstly, it is essential you revise somewhere where you feel comfortable. There should be no distractions, so turn the television off and put your mobile phone away. Do take regular breaks and ensure you eat regularly and drink plenty of water. This will help you concentrate.

Study skills

Research has shown that simply reading your notes or a textbook will not help you retain information. Look at the Learning Pyramid below. It illustrates various different methods of obtaining information and how likely it is you will retain it.

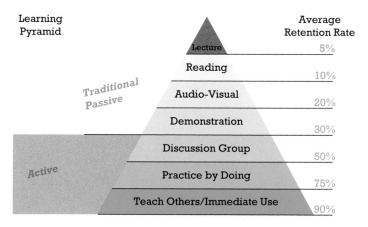

As you can see, you will only retain 10% of the information if you read it. Therefore, you must do something with the information in order to retain it. As shown in the diagram, discussing the information with a group or teaching others are the most effective ways. If this is not possible, simply saying the information aloud can be very helpful and a good way of testing what you have retained. The Modern Studies course is concerned with domestic and international events which are often the topic of conversation among adults and in social media forums. So join in a conversation when you can!

There are various ways to revise, these include:

- Rewriting class or textbook notes
- Summarising your notes
- Highlighting notes
- Making a revision flipper
- Writing revision cards
- Creating a mind map or spider diagram
- Writing questions to test yourself at a later date
- Completing past paper or exam practice questions
- Ask a friend or family member to ask you questions or discuss the subject with you
- Explain issues to someone else

Try to condense the information into a few words which should act as prompts to remind you of the information. This will help you to think about the information and evaluate or explain it in your extended response questions in the exam.

Learning summaries

Use the grids below to self-assess your knowledge in the relevant topics. Then make revision notes for each section of the Learning Summary which include relevant and up-to-date examples. Your revision notes could be spider-diagrams, mind maps, flippers, posters, lists, graphic organisers etc. Refer to these revision notes when completing practice exam questions.

Democracy in Scotland and the United Kingdom

Statement	Red	Amber	Green
Constitutional Arrangements			
I can describe reserved and devolved powers.			
I can explain the role and powers of the Scottish and/or UK governments.			
I can explain the changes to the role and powers of the Scottish and/or UK Parliaments.			
I can explain the powers of local government.			
I can explain the impact of the independence referendum.			
I can provide arguments for and against Scottish independence.			
I can explain the impact of EU decision making on the UK and/or Scotland.			
I can provide arguments for and against EU membership.			

Representative Democracy

I can explain the work of MSPs/MPs/MEPs and Local Councillors and provide examples.*			
I can describe the pressures on representatives from their political parties, constituents and pressure groups.			
I can describe how a bill becomes law in the Scottish and/or UK Parliaments.			
I can evaluate the work of committees in the Scottish Parliament and/or the second chamber in the UK Parliament.			
I can explain and evaluate the role and powers of the First Minister/Prime Minister.			
I can explain and evaluate the role and powers of the Cabinet.			
I can explain and evaluate the role and powers of the Civil Service.			
I can explain the ways the Scottish and/or UK government is held to account.			
I can describe the relationship between the UK and Scottish Parliaments.			
I can describe the relationship between the UK and/or Scottish Parliament and local councils.			

Voting Systems and Behaviour**

I can explain the arguments for and against FPTP in terms of representation, choice, fairness and complexity.			
I can explain the arguments for and against AMS in terms of representation, choice, fairness and complexity.			
I can explain the arguments for and against STV in terms of representation, choice, fairness and complexity.			
I can explain short- and long-terms factors which influence voting behaviour.			

Participation

I can explain the ways citizens influence the political system.			

Statement	Red	Amber	Green
I can explain and evaluate the influence of groups such as pressure groups or trade unions.			
I can explain and evaluate the role of the media in politics.			

* **Note**: You may have only been taught about one specific representative based on your chosen area of study.

** **Note**: You may have only been taught about one specific electoral system based on your chosen area of study.

Social Issues: Social Inequality in the United Kingdom

Statement	Red	Amber	Green
Social Inequality in the UK			
I understand the causes of inequality in regard to health, housing, family, educational attainment and income.			
I can provide evidence of social inequalities and make reference to geographical areas.			
Explanation and Theories of Inequality			
I can explain the debate between individualist and collectivist theories.			
I can show examples of collectivist theories in social welfare policies.			
I can show examples of individualist theories in social welfare policies.			
I can explain and provide examples of inequalities faced by women.			
I can explain and provide examples of inequalities faced by lone parents.			
I can explain and provide examples of inequalities faced by ethnic minorities.			
I can explain and provide examples of inequalities faced by the disabled.			
I can explain and provide examples of inequalities faced by the elderly.			
I can explain and provide examples of social mobility.			
Tackling Inequality			
I can describe current legislation aimed at tackling inequalities and evaluate its success.			

133

Statement	Red	Amber	Green
I can describe the benefits aimed at vulnerable groups and evaluate their success.			
I can explain the founding principles of the NHS and evaluate if the NHS operates within these principles today.			
I can explain the current issues and political opinion surrounding the NHS.			
I can explain the role and success of the third sector in reducing inequalities.			

Social Issues: Crime and the Law in the United Kingdom

Statement	Red	Amber	Green
The Role of Law in Society			
I understand some laws apply to different parts of the UK and can give examples of civil laws.			
I understand the rights granted to us as citizens of the UK and Europe.			
I understand the moral and legal responsibilities citizens have and can give examples of people who do not meet their social responsibilities.			
I can explain the difference between civil and criminal cases and can provide examples.			
I can describe how the police and courts are organised and operate.			
I can find and analyse recent crime statistics to give me an idea of the extent of crime in the UK.			
Theories and Causes of Crime			
I can explain the various causes of crime.			
I can describe, in detail, different theories of crime.			
The Impact of Crime on Society			
I can describe, in detail, the physical impact of crime.			
I can describe, in detail, the emotional effects of crime.			
I can describe, in detail, the financial impact of various types of crime.			

Statement	Red	Amber	Green
I can describe, in detail, the effect of crime on various vulnerable groups in society including children, the elderly, women and ethnic minorities.			
I can describe, in detail, the impact crime has on local communities.			
I can describe, in detail, the impact certain cases have had on UK politics.			

Tackling Crime

Statement	Red	Amber	Green
I can describe the different types of prisons in the UK.			
I can explain the aims of the penal system.			
I can assess information from various sources to conclude if the penal system is effective in meeting its aims for both society and the prisoners.			
I can outline the arguments in favour and against the use of private prisons.			
I can describe alternative methods of sentencing.			
I can analyse evidence to conclude if alternative methods of sentencing are successful.			
I can describe early intervention schemes.			

International Issues: World Power

Statement	Red	Amber	Green
Political System and Processes			
I can describe the rights and responsibilities granted to citizens in the world power I studied.			
I can explain the roles and functions of the executive, legislature and judiciary branches of government in the world power I studied.			
I can describe the role of the leader of the country and include relevant exemplification.			
I can describe the electoral system and process used to elect government officials in the world power I studied.			

Statement	Red	Amber	Green
I can explain a recent election result and its influence on the world power I studied.			
I can describe the various ways people can participate in politics and can provide relevant exemplification.			
I can explain and show evidence of political inequality in the world power I studied.			
I can evaluate the extent the government is held to account in the world power I studied.			
Socio-economic Inequalities			
I can describe the population demographic of the world power I studied.			
I can explain and provide evidence of inequalities between groups in society i.e. ethnic groups, gender groups and/or age groups.			
I can describe government policies and analyse their attempts to tackle inequalities in society.			
The Role of the World Power in International Relations			
I can explain the involvement the world power I have studied has on international organisations such as the UN, NATO, EU or African Union.			
I can describe and analyse the political, economic, military and/or humanitarian support the world power I have studied gives to other countries.			
I can summarise and evaluate the international power and influence of the world power I have studied.			

International Issues: A Significant World Issue

Statement	Red	Amber	Green
Causes of the Issue			
I can provide an overview of the scale of the world issue I have studied with relevant exemplification.			
I can explain the political and/or religious reasons for the issue.			
I can explain the social and economic reasons that cause or contribute to the world issue I have studied.			

Effects of the Issue

I can explain the effects of the issue on individuals in society.			
I can explain the effects of the issue on the country/ surrounding countries and their governments.			
I can explain the effects of the issue on a particular region of the world.			
I can explain the effects of the issue on the international community e.g the UN and military forces.			
Attempts to Resolve the World Issue			
I can describe the national attempts to resolve the world issue I have studied.			
I can describe the regional and/or international attempts to resolve the world issue I have studied.			
I can summarise and evaluate the success of the attempts to resolve the world issue I have studied.			

Glossary

Accountable: to hold completely responsible.

Administration: the people who are in the government.

Affiliate: an organisation controlled by or connected to another larger group.

Alliance: a group who agree to work together to achieve shared aims.

Assimilate: to become part of a country and society.

Asylum: protection or safety granted by a government to individuals who have been forced to leave their home country for their own safety.

Austerity: an economic situation caused by a reduction in government spending.

Autonomy: the ability to make your own decisions or self-govern without interference from anyone else.

Ballot: a system of confidential voting. A ballot paper is the piece of paper on which the electorate write their vote.

Barnett formula: the formula used by the UK government to determine the amount of money given to Scotland, Northern Ireland and Wales for public services. It is based on the population of each nation and the powers devolved to their administrations. It is controversial since different parts of the UK receive different amounts of money from the UK government. Typically, Scotland receives more money per person than England.

Benefit: financial assistance provided by the government to those in need or who qualify.

Biased: to favour something or someone unfairly by disregarding anything or anyone else.

Bureaucracy: complicated and time-consuming administrative procedures in government.

Candidate: a person who is competing for a job or elected position or is taking an exam.

Census: an official count of the number of people who live in a country and a collection of information about them.

Coalition: when two political parties join together to form or defeat the government.

Commission: a group of people formally chosen to carry out a significant piece of work or research.

Committee: a small group of people to represent a larger group. The group will carry out research and make decisions.

Compromise: to change your stance, opinion or demands in order to reach agreement with someone.

Consensus: a generally accepted opinion or decision among a group of people.

Constituency: the geographical area an MP or MSP represents in Parliament.

Council: a group of people elected to represent the views of a particular group of people, make decisions or give advice on a specialised subject.

Coup: a violent and illegal takeover of government power by the army.

Democracy: a system of government whereby the population vote for representatives to make decisions on their behalf.

Demographic: a group of people who are similar in some way.

Deploy: to use the military in an effective way and move soldiers and equipment to where they are needed.

Development: the process by which something grows or changes for the better.

Devolution: the transfer of power or responsibility from the main government to another, such as local government or the Scottish/Welsh or Northern Irish governments.

Devo-max: also known as full fiscal autonomy. A constitutional arrangement whereby the Scottish Parliament would receive all taxation levied in Scotland and use this to fund services in Scotland. The Scottish Parliament would no longer receive a block grant under the Barnett formula and would make payments to the UK government to contribute to the funding of UK-wide services.

Diplomacy/Diplomatic: managing relationships between countries and acting in a way that does not cause offence.

Discrimination: treating someone or a group of people negatively because of their race, gender, sexuality etc.

Economic migrant: a person who leaves their home country to live in another country in the hope they can earn more money and have a better standard of living.

Economy: the system of trade and business by which the wealth of a country is made and measured.

Embargo: to officially stop trading with another country.

Exaggeration: making something better, more important, worse etc than it really is.

Executive: the part of government responsible for making laws and putting decisions into practice.

Federal: a system of government whereby a group of regions are controlled by a central government.

Finance: relating to money, to manage or provide.

First Minister: the leader of the Scottish government.

Fiscal: relating to government revenue such as taxes.

Flagship: the best or most important.

Floating voter: a term used to describe a voter with no allegiances to one political party but who instead will choose who to vote for based on a number of short-term factors.

G20: the Group of Twenty, commonly referred to as the G20, are an international group of governments and bank governors from 20 major economies. They work together to achieve financial stability. The USA and UK are among the 20 members.

GDP: a way of measuring a country's wealth, taking into consideration the cost of living in that country.

Government: the group of people who run the country.

Holyrood: the Parliament building of the Scottish Government located in Edinburgh.

Ideology: a set of beliefs and ideas a group of people have, such as a political party.

Immigrant/Immigration: the movement of people from one country into another. You are an immigrant if you have left your home country to live in a different country.

Inclusion: to include someone or something. In relation to society, it is the idea that everyone should have access to the same facilities, activities and experiences without being disadvantaged. See **Social exclusion**.

Inequality: unequal. A situation in society were some have more than others e.g. money or opportunities.

Influence: to affect or change people's opinions or actions.

Institution: an organisation, custom or tradition that is an important part of society.

Intervene/Iintervention: to become involved to prevent a situation deteriorating.

Left-wing: a political term relating to one's beliefs. The political left is of the belief that

wealth and power should be shared more equally across groups in society.

Legislation: laws suggested by government and the process of making and enacting these.

Liberal/Liberalism: a set of political ideas based on equality and the freedom to live, work and travel.

Majority: more than half.

Manifesto: a statement of beliefs and intentions written by political parties.

Migrant/Migration: a person or the movement of people from one place or country to another, often to escape poverty and seek work.

Military: a country's armed forces e.g. army, navy and air force.

Minister: a member of government who is in charge of a particular responsibility e.g. the Minister of Education is responsible for the development and changes to education.

Minority: less than half. A small group.

Nuclear weapons: weapons which use the power of nuclear energy.

Opinion: thoughts or beliefs.

Opposition: the elected representatives of the largest political party that does not form the government.

Parliament: the group of elected representatives who make laws for the country.

Participation: to take part or become involved.

Partisan: strongly supporting a person, idea or political party.

Policy: a set of ideas or a plan.

Poll: to vote. Or a study in which people are asked their opinions.

Prejudice: an unfair assumption or opinion.

President: the title given to the person with the highest position in an organisation or government.

Pressure: to force or persuade.

Prime Minister: the leader of the government.

Principle: the basic idea of how something works. A standard of good behaviour.

Private sector: profit-seeking businesses that are not owned by government.

Privilege: an advantage that a person or group of people have.

Progressive: new ideas, social change, development. The system of progressive taxation is one in which the more money a person earns, the more tax they pay.

Proportional: in terms of representation, the number of votes relates to the number of representatives elected.

Proposal: a suggestion.

Public sector: businesses and industries controlled by the government.

Rebuttal: a statement to show an accusation or argument is untrue or invalid.

Recession: a period when a country's economy fails to make money and businesses struggle.

Recommendation: a suggestion.

Referendum: an election in which the electorate are asked a question to vote on. For example: Should Scotland become an independent country?

Represent/Representation: to act or speak on behalf of someone else.

Revolutionise: to completely change something for the better.

Right-wing: a political term relating to one's beliefs. The political right is of the belief that individuals take responsibility for their own wealth, not the government.

Sanction: a strong action to make a country obey international law. This is usually in the form of trade in which one country will stop trading with the other. This will prevent the country from making money.

Scrutinise/Scrutiny: to examine something in detail.

Secretary: an official or head of a government department.

Security: the protection of a person, building etc against threats or attacks.

Social exclusion: a situation in which some people who are poor or do not have a job do not feel part of the rest of society.

Social mobility: the ability to move from the lower class of society to a higher class.

Third sector: charities and voluntary organisations. Referred to as the third sector because government organisations (the public sector) and private companies (the private sector) are the first and second sectors of business.

Transferable: to move something or use something in a different situation.

Transparent: open and honest. Clear and easy to understand.

Treaty: a formal written agreement between two or more countries.

Veto: to forbid.

Welfare: help provided by the government in the form of benefits to those in need or who qualify.

Westminster: a borough of London where the UK Parliament building, the House of Commons, is found.

Working class: a group in society who earn little money and often do physical work.